*A Book Of*

# BUSINESS ETHICS

**For**
**BBA Semester - III (Course Code: 302)**
**As Per Pune University's Revised Syllabus**
**Effective from June 2014**

**Dr. B. H. AGALGATTI**
M. A., B. Com., L.L.B., M.B.A.,
Ph.D., F.I.I.I., Dip. (Trg. & Dev.),
P.G.D.M. (H.R.D.)

**Prof. S. KRISHNA**
M.A., L.L.B.

N2182

**B.B.A. : BUSINESS ETHICS (SEMESTER-III)**

**First Edition** : June 2014

© : Authors

ISBN 978-93-5164-032-5

The text of this publication, or any part thereof, should not be reproduced or transmitted in any form or stored in any computer storage system or device for distribution including photocopy, recording, taping or information retrieval system or reproduced on any disc, tape, perforated media or other information storage device etc., without the written permission of Authors th whom the rights are reserved. Breach of this condition is liable for legal action.

Every effort has been made to avoid errors or omissions in this publication. In spite of this, errors may have crept in. Any mistake, error or discrepancy so noted and shall be brought to our notice shall be taken care of in the next edition. It is notified that neither the publisher nor the author or seller shall be responsible for any damage or loss of action to any one, of any kind, in any manner, therefrom.

**Published By :**
**NIRALI PRAKASHAN**
Abhyudaya Pragati, 1312, Shivaji Nagar,
Off J.M. Road, PUNE – 411005
Tel - (020) 25512336/37/39, Fax - (020) 25511379
Email : niralipune@pragationline.com

**Printed By :**
Repro Knowledgecast Limited,
Thane

## DISTRIBUTION CENTRES
### PUNE

*Nirali Prakashan*
119, Budhwar Peth, Jogeshwari Mandir Lane
Pune 411002, Maharashtra
Tel : (020) 2445 2044, 66022708, Fax : (020) 2445 1538
Email : bookorder@pragationline.com

*Nirali Prakashan*
S. No. 28/27, Dhyari,
Near Pari Company, Pune 411041
Tel : (022) 24690371
Email : dhyari@pragationline.com
bookorder@pragationline.com

### MUMBAI
*Nirali Prakashan*
385, S.V.P. Road, Rasdhara Co-op. Hsg. Society Ltd.,
Girgaum, Mumbai 400004, Maharashtra
Tel : (022) 2385 6339 / 2386 9976, Fax : (022) 2386 9976
Email : niralimumbai@pragationline.com

## DISTRIBUTION BRANCHES

**NAGPUR**
*Pratibha Book Distributors*
Above Maratha Mandir, Shop No. 3, First Floor,
Rani Jhanshi Square, Sitabuldi, Nagpur 440012,
Maharashtra, Tel : (0712) 254 7129

**BENGALURU**
*Pragati Book House*
House No. 1, Sanjeevappa Lane, Avenue Road Cross,
Opp. Rice Church, Bengaluru – 560002.
Tel : (080) 64513344, 64513355,
Mob : 9880582331, 9845021552
Email:bharatsavla@yahoo.com

**JALGAON**
*Nirali Prakashan*
34, V. V. Golani Market, Navi Peth, Jalgaon 425001,
Maharashtra, Tel : (0257) 222 0395
Mob : 94234 91860

**KOLHAPUR**
*Nirali Prakashan*
New Mahadvar Road,
Kedar Plaza, 1st Floor Opp. IDBI Bank
Kolhapur 416 012, Maharashtra. Mob : 9855046155

### CHENNAI
*Pragati Books*
9/1, Montieth Road, Behind Taas Mahal, Egmore,
Chennai 600008 Tamil Nadu, Tel : (044) 6518 3535,
Mob : 94440 01782 / 98450 21552 / 98805 82331, Email : bharatsavla@yahoo.com

## RETAIL OUTLETS
### PUNE

*Pragati Book Centre*
157, Budhwar Peth, Opp. Ratan Talkies,
Pune 411002, Maharashtra
Tel : (020) 2445 8887 / 6602 2707, Fax : (020) 2445 8887

*Pragati Book Centre*
Amber Chamber, 28/A, Budhwar Peth,
Appa Balwant Chowk, Pune : 411002, Maharashtra,
Tel : (020) 20240335 / 66281669
Email : pbcpune@pragationline.com

*Pragati Book Centre*
676/B, Budhwar Peth, Opp. Jogeshwari Mandir,
Pune 411002, Maharashtra
Tel : (020) 6601 7784 / 6602 0855

*PBC Book Sellers & Stationers*
152, Budhwar Peth, Pune 411002, Maharashtra
Tel : (020) 2445 2254 / 6609 2463

### MUMBAI
*Pragati Book Corner*
Indira Niwas, 111 - A, Bhavani Shankar Road, Dadar (W), Mumbai 400028, Maharashtra
Tel : (022) 2422 3526 / 6662 5254, Email : pbcmumbai@pragationline.com

www.pragationline.com

info@pragationline.com

# Preface ...

We are happy to offer the present book entitled "**Business Ethics**" to our students and young scholars studying in the Under Graduate courses of Business Administration (BBA). This book is based on the newly revised syllabus of BBA Semester III effective from June 2014.

Great effort has been made here to present the salient features of Business Management in relation to applied ethics in everyday life. In these days of liberalisation, globalisation and privatisation, the role of business has become expanded to include onerous social responsibility and proactive economic developments. As such, only ethical business can become the engine for this change. A business manager who is steeped in ethical values will be a welcome harbinger of that golden era. It is to be hoped that the legal department of every corporation will have the assistance of a manager with deep commitment to and professional expertise in Business Ethics, to provide proper inputs and guidance to the Board of Management.

The authors are especially grateful to Dr. S. V. Kadavekar, Professor and Head of the Department of Commerce, and Research Centre, University of Pune, for his continued encouragement and valuable suggestions offered in his preface. He has spared his valuable time, erudition and experience generously for us.

The authors are always thankful to Prof. P. C. Shejwalkar, Dr. Sharad L. Joshi, Dr. V. V. Bhate, Dr. S. N. Kaushik, Dr. Mohan Kulkarni, Dr. D. K. Sinha, Prof. J. K. Oke and Prof. Manish R. Mundada, Pune. Dr. Ashok H. Chachadi, Karnataka University, Dharwar and Dr. S. A. Sidhanti, Regional Co-operative Management Institute, Bangalore, have always been a source of inspiration and support for quickening the process of writing and completing this book with timely reminders.

We thank **Smt Mukambika N. Nelli** and **Chi. Sau. Bhavana Guruprasad** and **Sri H. Guruprasad** as also **Chi. Bhooshan and Chi. Sau. Bhoomika** for their patience, love and moral support.

We thank our friends Shri Dineshbhai Furia, Shri Jignesh Furia and their staff for their excellent work in bringing out this book under the auspices of M/s Nirali Prakashan, Pune.

We welcome constructive comments and suggestions for improvement from our esteemed readers and student community.

**B. H. AGALGATTI**
**S. KRISHNA (NELLI)**

# Syllabus ...

1. **Introduction to Ethics**
   - Meaning and Nature of Ethics
   - Moral and Ethics
   - Importance of Ethics
   - Types of Ethics
   - Causes of Unethical Behaviour

2. **Areas of Business Ethics**
   - Meaning, Nature and Importance of Business Ethics
   - Types of Business Ethics
   - Factors Influencing Business Ethics
   - Corporate Ethics – Ethical Behavioiur and Audit of Ethical Behaviour
   - Individual Ethics, Professional Ethics
   - Gandhian Philosophy of Ethical Behaviour
   - Social Audit

3. **Business Ethics in a Global Economy**
   - Concept of Globalisation
   - Global Business Network
   - Relationship among Business, Business Ethics and Business Development
   - Developing Business Ethics in Global Economy
   - Marketing Ethics in Foreign Trade
   - Role of Business Ethics in Developing Civilised Society

4. **Moral Issues in Business**
   - Concept of Corporate Social Responsibility
   - Relationship between CSR and Business Ethics
   - Justice and Economic System Ethics Relating to Environment Protection
   - Business Ethics and Environment Protection
   - Business Ethics and Consumer Protection
   - Business Ethics and Social Justice
   - Arguments for and against Corporate Social Responsibility.

5. **Functional Ethics**
   - Meaning of Functional Ethics
   - Types of Ethics according to Functions of Business (Marketing, HRM, Purchase, Selling and Distribution)
   - Patents, Copy-rights, Intellectual Property Rights, Trade Marks and Business Ethics
   - Ethical Challenges for Managers in the 21$^{st}$ Century

•••

# Contents ...

1. Introduction to Ethics — 1.1 – 1.30

2. Areas of Business Ethics — 2.1 – 2.34

3. Business Ethics in a Global Economy — 3.1 – 3.26

4. Moral Issues in Business — 4.1 – 4.36

5. Functional Ethics — 5.1 – 5.16

   Case Studies — C.1 – C.4

•••

# Chapter 1...
# Introduction to Ethics

## Contents ...
1.1 Introduction
1.2 Meaning of Ethics
    1.2.1 Definitions of Ethics
    1.2.2 Nature of Ethics
    1.2.3 Moral and Ethics
    1.2.4 Importance of Ethics
    1.2.5 Types of Ethics
1.3 Causes of Unethical Behaviour
- Points to Remember
- Questions for Discussion

## Learning Objectives ...
- To learn about the meaning and nature of ethics
- To be aware of the concept of morals and ethics
- To gain knowledge of the importance and types of ethics
- To discuss the concept and nature of business ethics
- To closely examine the causes of unethical behaviour

## 1.1 Introduction

Ethics is not merely a classroom subject, nor ought to be so, in the most appropriate meaning of the term. Ethics is intrinsic to our daily life, and should be expressed in all our actions, speech, thought and attitude. It can be a subject of academic study only in order to make explicit moral principles and obligations inherent in every act.

We are, consciously or unconsciously, evaluating the actions of people around us and, as well as ourselves, and we frequently ask ourselves the question: 'Is it right or wrong? Is it good or bad? Does it give us happiness or sorrow?' We are all moral beings in the sense we are endowed with an acute sense of right and wrong, a sense of pride, contentment, and gladness in behaving properly and, a sense of shame, inadequacy and unhappiness when we behave improperly.

Although all people are endowed with an inborn moral sense, it is particularly the youth of a nation who are always found to be idealistic and implacably moral. It is they who are the first to understand the need for ecological protection, fair and just consumer practices, equitable and just treatment of employees, and the need for upholding human dignity and self-respect.

The post-Watergate era brought out successive exposes involving bribes and kickbacks, illegal political contributions, sale of defective tyres, spare parts for autos, Danken shield disaster, and so on. The ethnic relations brought up the issue of discrimination in employment, and on the other extreme, attempts to set this right gave place to the evil of 'reverse discrimination'. The exploitation of women, members of minorities, or religious and racial lines, caused no less ill-will. On the other hand, the tyranny of trade unionism in its worst aspect has been an evil not easy to rid of. The expansion of overseas corporate activities and the resulting trans-cultural activities of such MNCs have created moral problems to the corporations as well as the underdeveloped world.

All these issues cried for a moral solution. As a result, the people's attitude insofar as business changed, in the sense, that it demanded more demonstrable and quantifiable action in terms of social responsibility and positive contribution from the business community for the enrichment of life. The manager was the key to this new approach, as ownership of corporations had become divorced from its management. If the corporation had to be moral in its activities, it was the manager – or the individual - who was to take the ethical decision.

The significant part of a businessman's life, and it is also a large part of his life, is just business. In business, the people should be guided by concepts not only related to profitability and efficiency, but of professional integrity, responsibility, and fairness. The latter concepts demand an attention to ends and principles which have a universal application. In other words, morality governs the way we should live with each other and with ourselves.

The ethical manager of competent leadership should ask himself the following questions to seek a moral vision and purpose of his life's work:

(1) Can this system thrive apart from the moral culture that nourishes the virtues and values on which its existence depends?

(2) What are the appropriate goals for government, management and market?

(3) What is the corporation's purpose? To whom is it responsible? How are its legitimacy and authority derived?

(4) What are the responsibilities of the corporation towards the various stakeholders? How are these competing claims prioritised and weighed?

(5) How can managements establish a corporate context that is consistent with responsible, ethical decisions and actions?

(6) How important is the reputation of reliability, integrity, and fairness? How are the real interests of individuals and organisations best served in the long run by a systematic refusal to take short-term advantage?

(7) How should an individual decision-maker, when confronted with an ethical dilemma, reach a decision that is sound not only ethically and economically but also appropriate, competitive and effective?

Business ethics is as vast and as pervasive as business itself. The moral vision required can be acquired with moral imagination and a sympathetic understanding of the day to day occurrences in the business world around us. The subsequent paragraphs aim to present a broad theory of ethics and the general application of these principles to the dilemmas/problems that a manager may have to face and contend with successfully in the interest of both his organisation and peace of mind.

## 1.2 Meaning of Ethics

Ethics, or moral philosophy, is that branch of philosophy which has morality as its subject matter. Broadly speaking, it asks the question: 'What should we do? Obviously, the answer to 'what,' is determined and affected by 'We'. 'Should' and 'Do'. 'We' refers not to the disinterested or unconcerned observer, or a passive, or unaffected and reluctant individual, or a person who is weak-willed, biased, self-centred or irrational, or even the person who is not placed or positioned in the critical place of action.

It refers necessarily to a rational and responsible person who finds himself obliged and constrained to act by virtue of the position or office he occupies, and the function he is called upon to discharge. 'We' therefore refer to anyone called upon to act, and that person also happens to be a member of some identifiable socio-economic group. Or, simply put, it means the rational person obliged to act by virtue of his duty, situation, position or office.

'Should' indicates that it is a normative act. It is not what a person does or can do that is important, but what he 'ought' to do, that is the criterion of the act. What is good or bad, right or wrong, or, wise or unwise, would result from his act that is the crux of the matter. The third word 'do' is the indicator of the character of the doer. For character is knowledge (or wisdom) transmuted into action.

It is only by 'doing' that one's character is developed; that one's character is isolated; that one's character is revealed and defined. Character has an inseparable bearing on action. Thus, the 'what' in the question, 'What should we do?' has clearly not many and varied answers, although limited and defined by the answers to the position of the person called upon to act, his awareness of and a sense of responsibility towards the act, and his behavioural response determined by his character.

In a narrower sense of the term, 'ethics' is concerned with norms for the conduct of people as members of society. In this more specialised use of the term, ethics is referred to as 'morality'. Many attempts have been made to find, if possible, a set of moral principles or rules that would hold good for all rational people. However, a view prevails that such sets of rules can only be fairly specific to individual societies, at different periods of time. This leads to moral relativism.

### 1.2.1 Definitions of Ethics

1. *"Ethics is concerned not only with distinguishing right from wrong and good from bad but also with commitment to do what is right or what is good. The concept of ethics is inextricably linked to that of value, that is, an enduring belief that influences the choices we make from among available means and ends".*

    **Kenneth Kernaghan**
    **(Ethics in Public Service, – Ed R. A. Chapman – P. 15)**

2. *"Ethics is the art of human living and its result should be ease in being a good man in every circumstance".*

    **(Thomas Higgins, S. J., Basic Ethics, – P. 6 and 7)**

3. *"Ethics broadly and simply is the study of how our decisions affect other people. It is also the study of people's rights and duties and of the rules that people apply in making decisions."*

    **R. E. Freeman, A. F. Stoner, (Management – P. 116)**

4. *"Ethics are relative and not absolute – whether or not something is ethical behaviour depends on who is viewing and judging it. In general, we think ethical behaviour as a behaviour that conforms to the norms accepted by most of the society and unethical behaviour as behaviour that does not conform".*

    *Ethical (or unethical) behaviour is the result of a person's ethical (or unethical) decisions.*

    **(David D. Vanflect, (Behaviour in Organisation P. 241)**

5. *"Ethics is the inquiry concerned with the justification for person's actions. Such justification is the search for a coherent set of rules or norms which guide our actions when they cause conflict with others".*

    **R. Edward Feeman / Danniel R. Gilbert Jr.**
    **(Corporate Strategy and the Search for Ethics – P. 45)**

6. *"Ethics reflects the character of the individual and more contemporarily, perhaps, the character of the business firm, which is a collection of individuals".*

    **Wiley**

7. *"Ethics is concerned with the principles of good and evil, which are universal and eternal".*

   *"There is no special code of business ethics rather there are questions and dilemmas ...... Honesty, reliability, just and fair dealing are universally recognised as right, just as lying, cheating, stealing, cowardice and irresponsibility are recognised as wrong".*

   **Elizebeth Vallance,**

## 1.2.2 Nature of Ethics

According to Rituparna Raj, in her book "A Study in Business Ethics", the nature of ethics can be described as follows:

1. **Deals with Moral Judgement:** Ethics is an area dealing with moral judgement related to voluntary human conduct. Moral judgements require moral standards by which human behaviour is judged. It is these moral standards which are the ultimate end or the highest good for all concerned. Ethics therefore try to set the benchmark for the ultimate goal or the highest good to be achieved.

2. **Related to Humans only:** The idea of ethics is related to humans only as, it is only humans who have been gifted with the freedom of choice and the means of free will. Humans can distinguish between good and evil and right or wrong, just and proper.

3. **Systematic:** The study of ethics is a set of systematic knowledge about moral behaviour and conduct. The study of ethics is a science, a field of social science.

4. **Normative Science:** The science of ethics is a normative science. Normative sciences are concerned not with factual judgements but with judgements of what 'ought to be'. Thus, ethics is concerned with judgement of value or what ought to be. Ethics seeks to determine the nature of the norm, ideal or standard and seeks to enquire into the fitness of human actions to this ideal.

5. **Voluntary Human Conduct:** Ethics deals with human conduct which is voluntary and not enforced or coerced by people or circumstances.

6. **Descriptive:** Ethics are descriptive in their focus on moral situations.

7. **Focus on Human Values:** The focus in ethics is given to 'choice' of behaviour involving human values.

8. **Grounded in Interpretation, Perspective, and Cultural Beliefs:** Ethics are grounded in interpretation, perspective, and cultural beliefs. Often enacted, without consideration to the appropriateness or reasonableness of those beliefs.

9. **Systematic Knowledge:** Ethics aims at systematic knowledge. So, ethics is a science. Every science is concerned with a particular sphere of nature. As a science

ethics has its own particular sphere; it deals with certain judgements that we make about human conduct. It deals with systematic explanation of rightness or wrongness in the light of the highest Good of man.

10. **Not a Practical Science:** Practical science deals with means for the realisation of an end or ideal. It teaches us to know how to do. As for instance, medical science is a practical science. It concerns with the means in order to remove the causes of ailments or diseases. But ethics is not concerned with means in order to achieve moral ideal that is rightness or goodness. It does not teach us how to live a moral life. So, ethics cannot be regarded as a practical science.

11. **Not an Art:** Ethics does not teach us the art of leading a moral life. Rather it helps us to justify rightness or goodness which can lead to the supreme goal of human life that is to realise the *summum bonum* (the highest good) of human life. So, ethics is not a means to the highest ideal of human life. But, like the practical sciences, art is also a means for obtaining a goal. So, ethics is neither a practical science nor an art.

    Again the question is, is there any art of conduct? The reply is, in case of morality this is not true. Art especially deals with acquisition of skill to produce objects, while morality deals with motive, intention, purpose and choice which are considered right or wrong in the light of goodness. Therefore, morality consists of goodness, which is really an intrinsic end.

12. **Science of Values:** A norm or ideal in the ethical sense is defined as any regulatory principle that controls or lays guidelines to thought and mode of acting. Ethics is a science of values as it discovers the forms of conduct or behaviour.

    Ethics deals with moral phenomena and it observes and classifies them and explains them by the moral ideal. It distinguishes moral judgements from logical judgements and aesthetic judgements and reduced them to a system. So, we may define the nature of ethics as scientific. However, from another perspective all sciences also lead to philosophical questions if we take philosophy to be quest for knowledge. That is why ethics is a branch of philosophy.

### 1.2.3 Morals and Ethics

The meanings of morals and ethics overlap to some extent. Generally speaking, morals are personal or individual principles of right and wrong while a system of ethics deals with sets of those principles.

**Morals** and **morality** are about personal behaviour. Morals are principles or habits with respect to right or wrong conduct. It defines how things should work according to an individuals' ideals and principles.

Morals or the idea of morals presupposes the idea of a social rule. 'Social' refers to the whole of society, or of the society whose morality, it is; whereas 'rule' has a specific meaning, it rules out certain types of behaviour, and, rules, in certain other types. The latter types of rules are such that they are actively invoked and supported by the people who subject themselves to them.

In simple words, moral rules call upon the people (subject to them) to refrain from doing merely whatever they want. By 'social', we mean that its enforcement is totally social. Further, the moral rules are not enforced or legislated by a specific body of people designated or appointed for that purpose. That is law, not morals.

Morality is informal. Although there might not be any authoritative setting down of these rules, and there is no designated official enforcement, everyone (in society) participates in enforcing morality by praising, blaming, rewarding or punishing. In short, the morality of a society, therefore, is that set of rules or principles, or ideals which all rational members of that society accept, and apply to their own and other members' behaviour, and tend to reinforce the call for behaviour in others. To illustrate, the ethics of society 'M' is the set of rules which the members of 'M' do actually obey and actually attempt to get one another to conform to.

**Ethics** are the rules of conduct recognised in respect to a particular class of human actions or a particular group, culture, etc. It defines how things are according to the rules. Ethics are dependent on others for definition. They tend to be consistent within a certain context, but can vary between contexts. Ethics are governed by professional and legal guidelines within a particular time and place.

Ethics dictate the working of a social system. Ethics point towards the application of morality. Ethics lay down a set of codes that people must follow. Ethics are relative to peers, profession, community, society and nation. Ethics can be relatively simple to follow, while applying morals can be decidedly tougher. There can be a moral dilemma, but not an ethical one. While good morals represent correct and upright conduct, ethics act more as guidelines. Ethics are applicable or adhered to by a group or community or society, whereas morals relate to individuals.

| Basis of Difference | Ethics | Morals |
|---|---|---|
| **Meaning :** | The rules of conduct recognised in respect to a particular class of human actions or a particular group, culture, etc. It defines how thing are according to the rules. | Principles or habits with respect to right or wrong conduct. It defines how things should work according to an individuals' ideals and principles. |
| **Source :** | Social system - External | Individual - Internal |
| **Purpose :** | Because society says it is the right thing to do. | Because we believe in something being right or wrong. |
| **Consequences :** | If an individual does not function ethically, they may face societal disapproval and the goodwill will suffer. | Since morals have an internal source, a feeling of guilt and depression may occur. |
| **Flexibility :** | Ethics are dependent on others for definition. They tend to be consistent within a certain context, but can vary between contexts. | Usually consistent, although can change if an individual's beliefs change. |
| **Occurrence :** | A person strictly following Ethical Principles may not have any Morals at all. Likewise, one could violate Ethical Principles within a given system of rules in order to maintain Moral integrity. | A Moral Person although perhaps bound by a higher covenant, may choose to follow a code of ethics as it would apply to a system. "Make it fit" |
| **Origin :** | Greek word "ethos" meaning "character" | Latin words "mos" meaning "custom" and "moralities" meaning manner, character, and proper behaviour" |
| **Acceptability :** | Ethics are governed by professional and legal guidelines within a particular time and place | Morality is over and above the cultural norms. |

### 1.2.4 Importance of Ethics

Ethics is a moral code. It is the inner voice that tells a person what is right or wrong. Ethics can come from religion, from the law, from internal values, from learned values, from public opinion or from any number of sources. The whole of a person's ideas about morality and about what is right and wrong - and everything that goes into forming those ideas - determines what is and is not ethical.

Ethics is a requirement for human life. It is our means of deciding a course of action. Without it, our actions would be random and aimless. There would be no way to work towards a goal because there would be no way to pick between a limitless number of goals. Even with an ethical standard, we may be unable to pursue our goals with the possibility of success. To the degree which a rational ethical standard is taken, we are able to correctly organise our goals and actions to accomplish our most important values. Any flaw in our ethics will reduce our ability to be successful in our endeavours.

Ethics is the branch of study dealing with what is the proper course of action for man. It answers the question, "What do I do?" It is the study of right and wrong in human endeavours. At a more fundamental level, it is the method by which we categorise our values and pursue them.

1. Ethics are important because they allow society to continue to function. They are important because they help people to interact and live their daily lives in a functional way. They are important because they can govern a person's code of behaviour and prevent moral wrongs from occurring.

2. Ethics is an essential requirement for the smooth functioning of day to day human life.

3. Ethics is important because they keep people from doing what is wrong. If an individual has no ethics, he will do the wrong things whenever he believes it will benefit him and can get away with it.

4. Ethics are different than laws, and different than doing the right thing as a result of fear of consequences. While something that is unethical might be illegal, there is not necessarily a perfect overlap. Furthermore, in many ways, ethics can be even more important than the law, since the law will only deter a person from bad behaviour if he fears penalty, while a person with a strong code of ethics will do the right thing just because it is the right thing.

5. If a person had no code of ethics, he could steal, as long as no one is watching. He could lie to his loved ones or to strangers, as long as the lie does not rise to the level of criminal fraud. He could engage in all sorts of things that were 'wrong' and 'bad' as long as he did not get caught.

6. Since the law cannot possibly catch everyone each time they do something bad, and the law cannot make every 'wrong' action illegal, society would quickly fall apart if there were no ethical principles or moral rights or wrongs.

7. It is our means of deciding a course of action from various available options. Without it, our actions would be random and aimless.

8. There would be no way to work towards a goal because there would be no way to choose from a multitude of goals. Even with an ethical standard, we may not always be able to pursue our goals with the possibility of success. To the degree that we take a rational ethical standard, to that extent, are we able to correctly organise our goals and actions to accomplish our most important values.

9. Any flaw in our ethics will considerably reduce our ability to be successful in our endeavours.

10. We are social beings and we cannot survive without co-operation and joint endeavour. Ethics make sure that cooperation and joint endeavour run smoothly for the maximum collective benefit of all.

11. Ethics are important not only in business but in all aspects of life because it is an essential part of the foundation on which of a civilised society is built. A business or society that lacks ethical principles is bound to fail sooner or later.

### 1.2.5 Types of Ethics

Ethics is basically a branch of Philosophy. It concerns itself with the proper conduct and good living in the society. It lays emphasis on the principle of 'good life" which is satisfying.

There are many types of ethics, such as:
1. Normative Ethic
2. Meta-Ethics
3. Descriptive Ethics
4. Relational Ethics
5. Applied Ethics
6. Evolutionary Ethics

### 1.2.5.1 Normative Ethics

Ethics is about what ought to be, not what is. We simply would not need to consider what we ought to do if we always did it as a matter of course. Since we are focusing on morality and ethics, we are concerned with what morally ought to be the case. All ethical theories use various normative ethical principles in assessing or justifying actions and behaviour. To be practical and beneficial, ethical discourse must use understandings, procedures, and judgement criteria that all rational people who are concerned with morality and ethics must affirm. We need to understand that ethical principles must be the ground rules for our moral decision-making; they should not simply be factors we take into consideration. Normative ethics involves arriving at moral standards that regulate right and wrong conduct. In a sense, it is a search for an ideal test of proper behaviour. The Golden Rule is a classic example of a normative principle: "We should do unto others, what we would want others to do to us." Since I do not want my neighbour to steal my car, then, it is wrong for me to steal his car.

The key assumption in normative ethics is that there is only *one* ultimate criterion of moral conduct, whether it is a single rule or a set of principles. In this regard, three strategies will be noted, namely: (i) virtue theories, (ii) duty theories, and (iii) consequentialist theories.

**(i) Virtue Theory:** Many philosophers believe that morality consists of following precisely defined rules of conduct, such as, 'don't kill,' or 'don't steal.' Presumably, I must learn these rules, and then, make sure each of my actions live up to the rules. Virtue theorists, however, place less emphasis on learning rules, and instead stress the importance of developing good habits of character, such as, benevolence. Once I have acquired benevolence, for example, I will then habitually act in a benevolent manner. Plato emphasised four virtues in particular, which were later called cardinal virtues - wisdom, courage, temperance and justice. Other important virtues are - fortitude, generosity, self-respect, good temper, and sincerity.

**(ii) Duty or Deontological Theories :** Many of us feel that there are clear obligations we have as human beings, such as, to care for our children, and to not commit murder. Duty theories base morality on specific, foundational principles of obligation. These theories are sometimes called *deontological*, from the Greek word *deon*, or duty, in view of the foundational nature of our duty or obligation. They are also sometimes called *non-consequentialist* since, these principles are obligatory, irrespective of the consequences that might follow from our actions. For example, it is wrong to not care for our children even if it results in some great benefit, such as financial savings. There are four central duty theories.

The *first* is that championed by seventeenth century German philosopher, Samuel Pufendorf, who classified dozens of duties under three headings: duties to God, duties to oneself, and duties to others.

A second duty-based approach to ethics is rights theory. Most generally, a 'right' is a justified claim against another person's behaviour – such as, my right to not be harmed by you, as also enshrined in human rights. The rights and duties are related in such a way that the rights of one person imply the duties of another person.

A third duty-based theory is that of Kant, which emphasises a single principle of duty. Influenced by Pufendorf, Kant agreed that we have moral duties to oneself and others, such as, developing one's talents, and keeping our promises to others.

A fourth and more recent duty-based theory is that of British philosopher W. D. Ross, which emphasises *prima facie* duties. Like his seventeenth and eighteenth century counterparts, Ross argues that our duties are "part of the fundamental nature of the universe." However, Ross's list of duties is much shorter, which he believes reflects our actual moral convictions:

**Fidelity:** the duty to keep one's promises

**Reparation:** the duty to compensate others when we harm them

**Gratitude:** the duty to thank those who help us

**Justice:** the duty to recognise merit

**Beneficence:** the duty to improve the conditions of others

**Self-improvement:** the duty to improve our virtue and intelligence

**Non-maleficence:** the duty to not injure others

**(iii) Consequentialism/ Teleological Theories**: It is common for us to determine our moral responsibility by weighing the consequences of our actions. According to consequentialist normative theories, correct moral conduct is determined solely by a cost-benefit analysis of an action's consequences.

*"An action is morally right if the consequences of that action are more favourable than unfavourable."*

Consequentialist normative principles require that we first tally both the good and bad consequences of an action. Secondly, we then determine whether the total good consequences outweigh the total bad consequences. If the good consequences are greater, then, the action is morally proper. If the bad consequences are greater, then, the action is morally improper. Consequentialist theories are also called teleological theories, from the Greek word *telos*, or end, since the end result of the action is the sole determining factor of its morality.

In particular, competing consequentialist theories specify which consequences for affected groups of people are relevant. Thus, three sub-divisions of consequentialism emerge. They are:

**Ethical Egoism:** *"An action is morally right if the consequences of that action are more favourable than unfavourable only to the agent performing the action."*

**Ethical Altruism:** *"An action is morally right if the consequences of that action are more favourable than unfavourable to everyone except the agent."*

**Utilitarianism:** *"An action is morally right if the consequences of that action are more favourable than unfavourable to everyone."*

All these three theories focus on the consequences of actions for different groups of people. But, like all normative theories, the abovementioned three theories are rivals of each other. They also yield different conclusions. Consider the following example : A woman was travelling through a developing country when she witnessed a car in front of her run off the road and roll over several times. She asked the hired driver to pull over to assist but, to her surprise, the driver accelerated nervously past the scene. A few miles down the road, the driver explained that in his country if someone assists an accident victim, then, the police often hold the assisting person responsible for the accident itself. If the victim dies, then, the assisting person could be held responsible for the death. The driver continued explaining that road accident victims are, therefore, usually left unattended and often die from exposure to the country's harsh desert conditions. On the principle of ethical egoism, the woman in this illustration would only be concerned with the consequences of her attempted assistance as she would be affected. Clearly, the decision to drive on would be the morally proper choice.

On the principle of ethical altruism, she would be concerned only with the consequences of her action as others are affected, particularly the accident victim. Tallying only those consequences reveals that assisting the victim would be the morally correct choice, irrespective of the negative consequences that could result for her. On the principle of utilitarianism, she must consider the consequences for both herself and the victim. The outcome here is less clear, and the woman would need to precisely calculate the overall benefit versus non-benefit of her action.

### 1.2.5.2 Metaethics or Analytical Ethics

Metaethics is the most abstract area of moral philosophy. It does not ask what acts, or what kind of acts are good or bad, right or wrong; rather, it asks about the nature of goodness and badness, what it is to be morally right or wrong. The term 'meta' means after or beyond, and, consequently, the notion of metaethics involves a removed, or bird's eye view of the entire project of ethics. We may define metaethics as the study of the origin and meaning of ethical concepts. When compared to normative ethics and applied ethics, the field of metaethics is the least clearly defined area of moral philosophy.

**Moral Realism and Anti-realism**

Perhaps the biggest controversy in metaethics is that which divides moral realists and anti-realists.

**Moral realists** hold that moral facts are objective facts that are out there in the world. Things are good or bad independent of us, and then, we come along and discover morality.

**Anti-realists** hold that moral facts are not out there in the world until we put them there, that the facts about morality are determined by facts about us. On this view, morality is not something that we discover so much as something that we invent.

**Cognitivism and Non-cognitivism**

Closely related to the disagreement between moral realists and anti-realists is the disagreement between cognitivism and non-cognitivism. Cognitivism and non-cognitivism are theories of the meaning of moral statements.

According to **cognitivism**, moral statements describe the world. If I say that lying is wrong, then, according to the cognitivist, I have said something about the world, I have attributed the property 'wrongness' to an act lying. Whether lying has that property is an objective matter, and so my statement is objectively either true or false.

**Non-cognitivists**, on the other hand, disagree with this analysis of moral statements. According to non-cognitivists, when someone makes a moral statement they are not describing the world; rather, they are expressing their feelings or telling people what to do. Since non-cognitivism holds that moral statements are not descriptive, it entails that moral statements are neither true nor false. To be true is to describe something as being the way it is and, to be false is to describe something as being other than the way it is. The statements that are not descriptive cannot be either.

**Psychological Issues in Metaethics**

A second area of metaethics involves the psychological basis of our moral judgements and conduct, particularly, of understanding what motivates us to be moral. We might explore this subject by asking the simple question, "Why be moral?" Even if I am aware of basic moral standards, such as, eschewing from the acts of killing and stealing, this does not necessarily mean that I shall be psychologically compelled to act on them. Some answers to the question "Why be moral?" are to avoid punishment, to gain praise, to attain happiness, to be dignified, or to conform to societal norms.

(i) **Egoism and Altruism:** One important area of moral psychology concerns the inherent selfishness of humans. The seventeenth century British philosopher Thomas Hobbes held that many, if not all, of our actions are prompted by selfish desires. Even if an action seems selfless on the surface, such as, donating to charity, there could be selfish motives for doing so, namely, experiencing power over other people. This view is called psychological egoism and maintains that self-oriented interests ultimately motivate all human actions. Closely related to psychological egoism is a view called psychological hedonism which is the view that pleasure is the specific driving force behind all of our actions. The eighteenth century British philosopher Joseph Butler agreed that instinctive selfishness and pleasure prompt much of our conduct. However, Butler argued that we also have an inherent psychological capacity to show benevolence to others. This view is called psychological altruism which posits that at least some of our actions are motivated by instinctive benevolence.

(ii) **Emotion and Reason:** A second area of moral psychology involves a dispute concerning the role of reason in motivating moral actions. If, for example, I make the statement "abortion is morally wrong," am I making a rational assessment or only expressing my feelings? On the one side of the dispute, eighteenth century British philosopher David Hume argued that, moral assessments involve our emotions, and not our reason. We can amass all the reasons we want, but that alone will not constitute a moral assessment. We need a distinctly emotional reaction in order to make a moral pronouncement. The faculty of reason might be of service in giving us the relevant data, but, in Hume's words, "reason is, and ought to be, the slave of the passions." Inspired by Hume's anti-rationalist views, some twentieth century philosophers, most notably, A. J. Ayer, similarly denied that moral assessments are factual descriptions. For example, although the statement "it is good to donate to charity" may on the surface look as though it is a factual description about charity, it is not. Instead, a moral utterance like this involves two things. First, I (the speaker) am expressing my personal feelings of approval about charitable donations and I am in essence saying "Hooray for charity!" This is called the emotive element insofar as I am expressing my emotions about some specific behaviour. Secondly, I (the speaker) am trying to get you to donate to charity and am essentially giving the command, "Donate to charity!" This is called the prescriptive element in the sense that I am prescribing some specific behaviour.

From Hume's day forward, more rationally-minded philosophers have opposed these emotive theories of ethics and instead argued that moral assessments are indeed acts of reason. The eighteenth century German philosopher Immanuel Kant is a case in point. Although emotional factors often do influence our conduct, he argued, we should nevertheless resist that kind of sway. Instead, true moral action is motivated only by reason when it is free from emotions and desires. A recent rationalist approach, offered by Kurt Baier (1958), was proposed in direct opposition to the emotivist and prescriptivist theories of Ayer and others. Baier focuses more broadly on the reasoning and argumentation process that takes place when making moral choices. All of our moral choices are, or at least can be, backed by some reason or justification. If I claim that it is wrong to steal someone's car, then, I should be able to justify my claim with some kind of argument. For example, I could argue that stealing Smith's car is wrong since this would upset her, violate her ownership rights, or put the thief at risk of getting caught. According to Baier, then, proper moral decision-making involves giving the best reasons in support of one course of action versus another.

**(iii) Male and Female Morality:** A third area of moral psychology focuses on whether there is a distinctly female approach to ethics that is grounded in the psychological differences between man and woman. The discussions of this issue focus on two claims : (1) traditional morality is male-centered, and (2) there is a unique female perspective of the world which can be shaped into a value theory. According to many feminist philosophers, traditional morality is male-centered since it is modeled after practices that have been traditionally male-dominated, such as, acquiring property, engaging in business contracts, and governing societies. The rigid systems of rules required for trade and government were then taken as models for the creation of equally rigid systems of moral rules, such as, lists of rights and duties. Women, by contrast, have traditionally had a nurturing role, namely, that of raising children and overseeing domestic life. These tasks require less rule following, and more spontaneous and creative action. Therefore, if woman's experience is used as a role model for moral theory, then, it follows that the basis of morality would be spontaneous caring for others spontaneously caring for others as would be appropriate in each circumstance. On this model, the agent becomes part of the situation and acts caringly within that context. This stands in contrast with male-modeled morality where the agent is a mechanical actor who performs his required duty, but can remain distanced from and unaffected by the situation. A care-based approach to morality, as it is sometimes called, is offered by feminist ethicists as either a replacement for or a supplement to traditional male-modeled moral systems.

### 1.2.5.3 Descriptive Ethics

The category of normative ethics involves creating or evaluating moral standards. Thus, it is an attempt to figure out what people should do or whether or not their current moral behaviour is reasonable. Traditionally, most of the field of moral philosophy has involved normative ethics - there are few philosophers out there who have not tried their hand at explaining what they think people should do and why.

Descriptive ethics is sometimes referred to as comparative ethics because so much activity can involve comparing ethical systems: comparing the ethics of the past to the present, comparing the ethics of one society to another and comparing the ethics which people claim to follow with the actual rules of conduct which do describe their actions.

Strictly speaking, then, descriptive ethics is not entirely a field within philosophy - rather, it is more a specialty which involves many different fields within the social sciences. It is neither designed to provide guidance to people in making moral decisions nor is it designed to evaluate the reasonableness of moral norms. Nevertheless, actual work in moral philosophy cannot proceed very far without the knowledge gained from descriptive ethics.

In short, descriptive ethics asks these two questions:

1. What do people claim as their moral norms?
2. How do people actually behave when it comes to moral problems?

### 1.2.5.4 Relativism Ethics

What is ethical relativism? Relativism is the position that all points of view are equally valid and the individual determines what is true and relative for them. Relativism theorises that truth is different for different people, not simply that different people believe different things to be true. While there are relativists in science and mathematics, ethical relativism is the most common variety of relativism. Almost everyone has heard a relativist slogan:

What's right for you may not be what's right for me.

What's right for my culture won't necessarily be what's right for your culture.

No moral principles are true for all people at all times and in all places.

Ethical relativism represents the position that there are no moral rights or wrongs in the absolute sense. This position would assert that our morals evolve and change with social norms over a period of time. This philosophy allows people to mutate ethically as the culture, knowledge, and technology change in society. Slavery is a good example of ethical relativism. Repeatedly the value of a human being is determined by a combination of social preferences and patterns, experience, emotions, and rules that seemed to bring about the most benefit.

What is ethical relativism from a subjective view? Subjective ethical relativism supports the view that the truth of moral principles is relative to individuals. Whatever you believe is right for you personally is completely up to you to determine. Subjective relativism allows you to be sovereign over the principles that dictate how you live your life.

Conventional ethical relativism supports the view that the truth of moral principles is relative to cultures. Unlike the subjective view, what is right for you as an individual is dependent upon what your particular culture believes is right for you. This view supports the concept that whatever culture says is right for you really is right for you. The culture or society becomes the highest authority about what is right for each individual within that society. Thus, conventional relativism places the individual's will subordinate to the will of the cultural majority.

What is ethical relativism from an absolute view? The desire to have an absolute set of ethics implies an Absolute Ethics Source which can easily be deduced as being God. This position would be opposed to ethical relativism. Instead, the relativist excludes any religious system based on absolute morals and would condemn absolute ethics. God has the power to convey things to us that are absolute, truthful and ethical. Those absolutes, however, may not be to our liking or please our subjective tastes. To quote the Bible : "'For my thoughts are not your thoughts, neither are your ways my ways,' declares the Lord" (Isaiah 55:8).

Therefore, relying on an individual's or a society's moral choices is analogous to using our sense of touch to determine the extent of a child's fever. When a child is sick, a more precise and consistent measurement is imperative. Our mental growth and the health of our soul is also worthy of a more accurate gauge than subjective human feelings. Conventional relativism implies that all you have to do is convince a few of your close friends to engage in some activity that is viewed as immoral by the rest of society. Suddenly you have now made the previously unacceptable activity ethically and morally correct for you. "There is a way that seems right to a man, but in the end it leads to death".

### 1.2.5.5 Applied Ethics

Applied ethics is the branch of ethics which consists of the analysis of specific, controversial moral issues, such as, abortion, animal rights, or euthanasia. In recent years, applied ethical issues have been subdivided into convenient groups, such as, medical ethics, business ethics, environmental ethics, and sexual ethics. Generally speaking, two features are necessary for an issue to be considered an 'applied ethical issue.' First, the issue needs to be controversial in the sense that there are significant groups of people both for and against the issue at hand. The issue of drive-by shooting, for example, is not an applied ethical issue, since everyone agrees that this practice is grossly immoral. By contrast, the issue of gun control would be an applied ethical issue since there are significant groups of people both for and against gun control.

The second requirement for an issue to be an applied ethical issue is that it must be a distinctly moral issue. On any given day, the media presents us with an array of sensitive issues, such as, affirmative action policies, homosexuals in the military, involuntary commitment of the mentally impaired, capitalistic versus socialistic business practices, public versus private health care systems, or energy conservation. Although all of these issues are controversial and have an important impact on society, all of them are not moral issues. Some are only issues of social policy. The aim of social policy is to help make a given society run efficiently by devising conventions, such as, traffic laws, tax laws, and zoning codes. Moral issues, by contrast, concern more universally obligatory practices, such as, our duty to avoid lying, and are not confined to individual societies. Frequently, the issues of social policy and morality overlap, as with murder which is both socially prohibited and immoral. However, the two groups of issues are often distinct. For example, many people would argue that sexual promiscuity is immoral, but may not feel that there should be social policies regulating sexual conduct, or laws punishing promiscuity. Similarly, some social policies forbid residents in certain neighbourhoods from having yard sales. But, so long as the neighbours are not offended, there is nothing immoral in itself about a resident having a yard sale in one of these neighbourhoods. Thus, to qualify as an applied ethical issue, the issue must be more than one of mere social policy, it must be morally relevant as well.

In theory, resolving particular applied ethical issues should be easy. With the issue of abortion, for example, we would simply determine its morality by consulting our normative principle of choice, such as, act-utilitarianism. If a given abortion produces greater benefit than disbenefit, then, according to act-utilitarianism, it would be morally acceptable to have the abortion. Unfortunately, there are perhaps hundreds of rival normative principles from which to choose, many of which yield opposite conclusions. Thus, the stalemate in normative ethics between conflicting theories prevents us from using a single decisive procedure for determining the morality of a specific issue. The usual solution today to this stalemate is to consult several representative normative principles on a given issue and see where the weight of the evidence lies.

**(i) Normative Principles in Applied Ethics:** The task of arriving at a short list of representative normative principles is itself a challenging task. The principles selected must not be too narrowly focused, such as, a version of act-egoism that might focus only on an action's short-term benefit. The principles must also be seen as having merit by people on both sides of an applied ethical issue. For this reason, principles that appeal to duty to God are not usually cited since this would have no impact on a non-believer engaged in the debate. The following principles are the ones most commonly appealed to in applied ethical discussions:

- **Personal Benefit:** Acknowledge the extent to which an action produces beneficial consequences for the individual in question.
- **Social Benefit:** Acknowledge the extent to which an action produces beneficial consequences for society.
- **Principle of Benevolence:** Help those in need.
- **Principle of Paternalism:** Assist others in pursuing their best interests when they cannot do so themselves.
- **Principle of Non-harm/Non-violence:** Do not harm others.
- **Principle of Honesty:** Do not deceive others.
- **Principle of Lawfulness:** Do not violate the law.
- **Principle of Autonomy:** Acknowledge a person's freedom over his/her actions or physical body.
- **Principle of Justice:** Acknowledge a person's right to due process, fair compensation for harm/damages undergone and fair distribution of benefits.
- **Rights:** Acknowledge a person's rights to life, information, privacy, free expression, and safety.

The above principles represent a spectrum of traditional normative principles and are derived from both consequentialist and duty-based approaches. The first two principles, personal benefit and social benefit, are consequentialist since they appeal to the consequences of an action as it affects the individual or society. The remaining principles are duty-based. The principles of benevolence, paternalism, non-harm, honesty, and lawfulness are based on duties we have toward others. The principles of autonomy, justice, and the various rights are based on moral rights.

An example will help illustrate the function of these principles in an applied ethical discussion. In 1982, a couple from Bloomington, Indiana, gave birth to a baby with severe mental and physical disabilities. Among other complications, the infant, known as Baby Doe, had its stomach disconnected from its throat and was thus unable to receive nourishment. Although this stomach deformity was correctable through surgery, the couple did not want to raise a severely disabled child and, therefore, chose to deny surgery, food, and water for the infant. Local courts supported the parents' decision, and six days later Baby Doe died. Should corrective surgery have been performed for Baby Doe? Arguments in favour of corrective surgery derive from the infant's right to life and the principle of paternalism which stipulates that we should pursue the best interests of others when they are incapable of doing so themselves. Arguments against corrective surgery derive from the personal and social disbenefit which would result from such surgery. If Baby Doe survived, its quality of life would have been poor and, in any case, it probably would have died at an early age. Also, from the parent's perspective, Baby Doe's survival would have been a significant emotional and financial burden. When examining both sides of the issue, the parents and the courts concluded that the arguments against surgery were stronger than the arguments for surgery. First, foregoing surgery appeared to be in the best interests of the infant, given the poor quality of life it would endure. Second, the status of Baby Doe's right to life was not clear given the severity of the infant's mental impairment. For, to possess moral rights, it takes more than merely having a human body, certain cognitive functions must also be present. The issue here involves what is often referred to as moral personhood, and is central to many applied ethical discussions.

**(ii) Issues in Applied Ethics:** There are many controversial issues discussed by ethicists today, some of which will be briefly mentioned here.

Biomedical ethics focuses on a range of issues which arise in clinical settings. Health care workers are in an unusual position of continually dealing with life and death situations. Pre-natal issues arise about the morality of surrogate mothering, genetic manipulation of foetuses, the status of unused frozen embryos, and abortion. Other issues arise about patient rights and physician's responsibilities, such as, the confidentiality of the patient's records and the physician's responsibility to tell the truth to dying patients. The AIDS crisis has raised the specific issues of the mandatory screening of all patients for AIDS, and whether physicians can refuse to treat AIDS patients. That apart, additional issues concern medical experimentation on humans, the morality of involuntary commitment, and the rights of the mentally disabled. Finally, the right to end of life raises the issue about the morality of suicide, the justifiability of suicide intervention, physician-assisted suicide, and euthanasia.

The field of business ethics examines moral controversies relating to the social responsibilities of capitalist business practices, the moral status of corporate entities, deceptive advertising, insider trading, basic employee rights, job discrimination, affirmative action, drug testing, and whistle-blowing.

Most often, issues in environmental ethics often overlap with business and medical issues. These include the rights of animals, the morality of animal experimentation, preserving endangered species, pollution control, management of environmental resources, whether eco-systems are entitled to direct moral consideration, and our obligation to future generations.

That apart, controversial issues of sexual morality, include - monogamy versus polygamy, sexual relations without love, homosexual relations, and extra-marital affairs.

Finally, there are issues of social morality which examine capital punishment, nuclear war, gun control, use of drugs for recreational purposes, welfare rights, and racism.

## Benefits of Applied Ethics

This means that practical ethics disallows neutrality in resolving morally dilemmic issues. A constant application of practical methods of ethical analysis offers several benefits to the manager and makes him see things more holistically.

1. It enables him to develop the skill to recognise moral issues clearly. Those issues which involve the rights and/or welfare of persons, the character of the acting agent, the flourishing of relationships and communities, special obligations attached to special roles, and so on, are the issues which have a moral content. For instance, the finding of unjust manipulative or even coercive veins even in standard business behaviours would invariably require one to be morally awake and alert. As a positive spin-off, such activity raises one's consciousness to a higher moral plane.

2. He will be able to develop his moral imagination. This means that issues whose moral aspect is taken for granted, or accepted with indifference, take on a moral dimension on closer view, by putting oneself in the place of the subject or victim. Such are issues concerning oppression and/or discrimination against women or members of certain minorities, senior citizens, or child labour, and so on.

   One must be able to assume the place and role of the worker, who may be desperate for work, bored and frustrated, confused by complex machinery, feeling displaced and unwanted, to realise his outlook and moral apprehension. This moral imagination gives rise to ethical insight, which is the faculty that enables one to distinguish false or irrational convictions or assumptions from correct and rational ones.

3. The third and more lasting benefit is the sharpening of the analytical and critical skills of the decision-maker. Although moral relativism is an acceptable part of reality, caution induced by that outlook must be carefully reined in and controlled. To be sure, calling another person's action morally wrong does amount to a strong and important claim.

   Thus far, establishing exact and unquestionable criteria for moral rightness has proved to be an elusive task. But, he should not let this impossibility induce in him (the decision-maker), a sense of hapless subjectivism. It is all too easy to adopt the attitude of 'Judge not, lest thou be judged', and wear the mask of smug tolerance and benign neutrality. Unfortunately, excessive tolerance erodes self-confidence and clouds moral vision, and makes the decision-maker sink into inept passivity and idle permissibility. It is necessary to accept the reality that although moral questions are difficult (if they were not difficult, would they necessitate resolution?) it is worthwhile and even obligatory to confront them and analyse them as far as human ingenuity can go.

   By honing our analytical skills, we see that a large common moral ground is uncovered and can be defended on the basis of reasonable moral principles. A careful and consistent moral reasoning will reveal that some potential resolutions were not in conformity with moral principles or, that an irresolvable issue did actually possess a simple procedural resolution.

## 1.2.5.6 Evolutionary Ethics

Evolutionary ethics tries to bridge the gap between philosophy and the natural sciences by arguing that natural selection has instilled human beings with a moral sense, a disposition to be good. If this were true, morality could be understood as a phenomenon that arises automatically during the evolution of sociable, intelligent beings and not, as theologians or philosophers might argue, as the result of divine revelation or the application of our rational faculties.

Morality would be interpreted as a useful adaptation that increases the fitness of its holders by providing a selective advantage. This is certainly the view of Edward O. Wilson, the 'father of sociobiology', who believes that *"scientists and humanists should consider together the possibility that the time has come for ethics to be removed temporarily from the hands of the philosophers and biologicised"* **(Wilson, 1975: 27)**. The challenge for evolutionary biologists, such as, Wilson is to define goodness with reference to evolutionary theory and then explain why human beings ought to be good.

### (i) Key Figures and Key Concepts

### (a) Charles Darwin

The biologisation of ethics started with the publication of *The Descent of Man* by Charles Darwin (1809-1882) in 1871. In this follow-up to *On the Origin of Species*, Darwin applied his ideas about evolutionary development to human beings. He argued that humans must have descended from a less highly organised form – in fact, from a "hairy, tailed quadruped inhabitant of the Old World" (Darwin, 1930: 231). The main difficulty Darwin saw with this explanation is the high standard of moral qualities apparent in humans. To decode this puzzle, Darwin devoted a large chapter of the book to evolutionary explanations of the moral sense, which he argued must have evolved in two main steps.

First, the root for human morality lies in the social instincts. Building on this claim by Darwin, today's biologists would explain this as follows. Sociability is a trait whose phylogenetic origins can be traced back to the time when birds 'invented' brooding, hatching, and caring for young hatchlings. To render human beings to be able to fulfil parental responsibilities required social mechanisms unnecessary at earlier stages of evolutionary history. For example, neither amoebae (which reproduce by division) nor frogs (which leave their tadpole-offspring to fend for themselves) need the social instincts present in birds. At the same time as facilitating the raising of offspring, social instincts counterbalanced innate aggression. It became possible to distinguish between 'them' and 'us' and aim aggression towards individuals that did not belong to one's group. This behaviour is clearly adaptive in the sense of ensuring the survival of one's family.

Secondly, with the development of intellectual faculties, the human beings were able to reflect on past actions and their motives and thus approve or disapprove of others as well as themselves. This led to the development of a conscience which became the supreme judge and monitor' of all actions. Being influenced by utilitarianism, Darwin believed that the greatest-happiness principle will inevitably come to be regarded as a standard for right and wrong by social beings with highly evolved intellectual capacities and a conscience.

Based on these claims, can Darwin answer the two essential questions in ethics? First, how can we distinguish between 'good' and 'evil'? And second, why should we be good? If all his claims were true, they would indeed support answers to the above questions. Darwin's distinction between good and evil is identical with the distinction made by hedonistic utilitarians. Darwin accepts the greatest-happiness principle as a standard of right and wrong. Hence, an action can be judged as good if it improves the greatest happiness of the greatest number, by either increasing pleasure or decreasing pain. And the second question – why we should be good – does not pose itself for Darwin with the same urgency as it did, for instance, for Plato (Thrasymachus famously asked Socrates in the *Republic* why the strong, who are not in need of aid, should accept the Golden Rule as a directive for action). Darwin would say that humans are biologically inclined to be sympathetic, altruistic, and moral as this proved to be an advantage in the struggle for existence.

### (b) Herbert Spencer

The next important contribution to evolutionary ethics was by Herbert Spencer (1820-1903), the most fervent defender of that theory and the creator of the theory of Social Darwinism. Spencer's theory can be summarised in three steps. As did Darwin, Spencer too believed in the theory of hedonistic utilitarianism as proposed by Jeremy Bentham and John Stuart Mill. In his view, gaining pleasure and avoiding pain directs all human action. Hence, moral good can be equated with facilitating human pleasure. Second, pleasure can be achieved in two ways, first by satisfying self-regarding impulses and second by satisfying other-regarding impulses. This means that eating one's favourite food and giving food to others are both pleasurable experiences for humans. Third, mutual co-operation between humans is required to coordinate self and other-regarding impulses, which is why humans develop principles of equity to bring altruistic and egoistic traits into balance (Fieser, 2001 : 214).

However, Spencer did not become known for his theory of mutual co-operation. On the contrary, his account of Social Darwinism is contentious todate because it is mostly understood as "an apology for some of the most vile social systems that humankind has ever perpetrated," for instance, German Nazism (Ruse, 1995 : 228). In short, Spencer elevated alleged biological facts (struggle for existence, natural selection, survival of the fittest) to prescriptions for moral conduct. For instance, he suggested that life is a struggle for human beings, and that, in order for the best to survive, it is necessary to pursue a policy of non-aid for the weak: "to aid the bad in multiplying, is, in effect, the same as maliciously providing for our descendants a multitude of enemies." (Spencer, 1874 : 346). Spencer's philosophy was widely popular, particularly, in North America in the nineteenth century, but declined significantly in the twentieth century.

Which answers could he give to the two essential questions in ethics? How can we distinguish between good and evil and why should we be good? Spencer's answer to question one is identical to Darwin's as they both supported hedonistic utilitarianism. However, his answer to question two is interesting, if untenable. Spencer alleged that evolution equalled progress for the better (in the moral sense of the word) and that anything which supported evolutionary forces would therefore be good (Maxwell, 1984 : 231). The reasoning behind this was that nature shows us what is good by moving towards it; and hence, "evolution is a process which, in itself, generates value" (Ruse, 1995 : 231). If evolution advances the moral good, we ought to support for our self-interest. Moral good was previously identified with universal human pleasure and happiness by Spencer. If the evolutionary process directs us towards this universal pleasure, we have an egoistic reason for being moral, namely, that we want universal happiness. However, to equate development with moral progress for the better was a major value judgement which cannot be held without further evidence, and most evolutionary theorists have given up on the claim (Ruse, 1995: 233; Woolcock, 1999: 299). It also is subject to more conceptual objections, namely, deriving 'ought" from 'is,' and committing the naturalistic fallacy.

### (c) The Is-Ought Problem

The first philosopher who persistently argued that normative rules cannot be derived from empirical facts was David Hume (1711-1776) (1978 : 469)

In every system of morality, which I have hitherto met with, I have always remarked, that the author proceeds for some time in the ordinary way of reasoning, and establishes the being of a God or makes observations concerning human affairs; when all of a sudden I am surprised to find, that instead of the usual copulations of propositions, *is*, and *is not*, I meet with no proposition that is not connected with an *ought*, or an *ought not*. This change is imperceptible; but is, however, of the last consequence.

It is this unexplained, imperceptible change from 'is' to 'ought' which Hume deplores in moral systems. To say, what *'is'* the case and to say what *'ought to be'* the case are two unrelated matters, according to him. On the one hand, empirical facts do not contain normative statements; otherwise they would not be purely empirical. On the other hand, if there are no normative elements in the facts, they cannot suddenly surface in the conclusions because a conclusion is only deductively valid if all necessary information is present in the premises.

How do Darwin and Spencer derive 'ought' from 'is'? Let us look at Darwin first, using an example which he could have supported.

Child 'A' is dying from starvation.

The parents of child 'A' are not in a position to feed their child.

The parents of child 'A' are very unhappy that their child is dying from starvation.

Therefore, fellow humans ought morally to provide food for child 'A'.

Darwin (1930: 234) writes that "happiness is an essential part of the general good." Therefore, those who want to be moral ought to promote happiness, and hence, in the above case, provide food. However, the imperceptible move from 'is' to 'ought' which Hume found in moral systems, is also present in this example. Thus, Darwin derives 'ought' from 'is' when he moves from the empirical fact of unhappiness to the normative claim of a duty to relieve unhappiness.

The same can be said for Spencer whose above argument about the survival of the fittest could be represented as follows:

Natural selection will ensure the survival of the fittest.

Person 'B' is dying from starvation because he is ill, old, and poor.

Therefore, fellow humans ought to morally avoid helping the person 'B' so that the survival of the fittest is guaranteed.

Even if both premises were shown to be true, it does not follow that we *ought* to morally support the survival of the fittest. An additional normative claim equating survival skills with moral goodness would be required to make the argument tenable. Again, this normative part of the argument is not included in the premises. Hence, Spencer also derives 'ought' from 'is.' Thomas Huxley (1906: 80) objects to evolutionary ethics on these grounds when he writes:

"The thief and the murderer follow nature just as much as the philantropist. Cosmic evolution may teach us how the good and the evil tendencies of man may have come about; but, in itself, it is incompetent to furnish any better reason why what we call good is preferable to what we call evil than we had before.

### (d) The Naturalistic Fallacy

But evolutionary ethics was not only attacked by those who supported Hume's claim that normative statements cannot be derived from empirical facts. A related argument against evolutionary ethics was voiced by British philosopher G.E. Moore (1873-1958). In 1903, he published a ground-breaking book, *Principia Ethica*, which created one of the most challenging problems for evolutionary ethics: the 'naturalistic fallacy.' According to Michael Ruse (1995), when dealing with evolutionary ethics, "it has been enough for the student to murmur the magical phrase 'naturalistic fallacy,' and then, he or she can move on to the next question, confident of having gained full marks thus far on the exam". So, what is the naturalistic fallacy and why does it pose a problem for evolutionary ethics?

Moore was interested in the definition of 'good' and, particularly, in whether the property *good* is simple or complex. Simple properties, according to Moore, are indefinable as they cannot be described further using more basic properties. Complex properties, on the other hand, can be defined by outlining their basic properties. Hence, the colour 'yellow' cannot be defined in terms of its constituent parts; whereas 'coloured' can be explained further as it consists of several individual colours.

'Good,' according to Moore, is a simple property which cannot be described using more basic properties. Committing the naturalistic fallacy is attempting to define 'good' with reference to other natural, i.e., empirically verifiable, properties. This understanding of 'good' creates serious problems for both Darwin and Spencer. Following Bentham and Mill, both identify moral goodness with 'pleasure.' This means they commit the naturalistic fallacy as good and pleasant are not identical. In addition, Spencer identifies goodness with 'highly evolved,' committing the naturalistic fallacy again. (Both Moore's claim in itself as well as his criticism of evolutionary ethics could be countered, but this would fall outside the scope of this topic under discussion.)

### (e) Sociobiology

Despite the continuing challenge of the naturalistic fallacy, evolutionary ethics has moved on with the advent of sociobiology. In 1948, at a conference in New York, scientists decided to initiate new inter-disciplinary research between zoologists and sociologists. 'Sociobiology' was the name given to the new discipline aiming to find universally valid regularities in the social behaviour of animals and humans. Here, emphasis was put on the study of biological, i.e., non-cultural, behaviour. The field did, however, not get off the ground until Edward Wilson published his *Sociobiology: The New Synthesis* in 1975. According to Wilson, (1975: 4), "sociobiology is defined as the systematic study of the biological basis of all social behaviour."

In Wilson's view, sociobiology makes philosophers, redundant, at least temporarily, especially, when it comes to questions of ethics. He believes that ethics can be explained biologically when he writes.

The hypothalamus and limbic system ... flood our consciousness with all the emotions – hate, love, guilt, fear, and others – that are consulted by ethical philosophers who wish to intuit the standards of good and evil. What, we are then compelled to ask made the hypothalamus and the limbic system? The answer to the aforesaid question is that they evolved by natural selection. That simple biological statement must be pursued to *explain ethics*.

Ethics, following this understanding, evolved under the pressure of natural selection. Sociability, altruism, cooperation, mutual aid, etc., are all explicable in terms of the biological roots of human social behaviour. Moral conduct aided the long-term survival of the morally inclined species of humans. According to Wilson (ibid. 175), the prevalence of egoistic individuals will make a community vulnerable and ultimately lead to the extinction of the whole group. Mary Midgley agrees. In her view, egoism pays very badly in genetic terms, and a "consistently egoistic species would be either solitary or extinct" (Midgley, 1980 : 94).

Wilson avoids the naturalistic fallacy in *Sociobiology* by not equating goodness with another natural property, such as, pleasantness, as Darwin did. This means that he does not give an answer to our first essential question in ethics. What is good? However, like Darwin he gives an answer to the second question. Why should we be moral? We are moral because we are genetically inclined to be so. It is a heritage of earlier times when less morally inclined and more morally inclined species came under pressure from natural selection. Hence, we do not need divine revelation or strong will to be good; we are simply genetically wired to be good. The emphasis in this answer is not on the word 'should', as it is not our free will which makes us decide to be good but our genetic heritage.

One of the main problems evolutionary ethics faces is that ethics is not a single field with a single quest. Instead, it can be separated into various areas, and evolutionary ethics might not be able to contribute to all of them. Let us therefore look at a possible classification of evolutionary ethics, which maps it on the field of traditional ethics, before concluding with possible criticisms.

## (ii) Placement in Contemporary Ethical Theory

For philosophy students, ethics is usually divided into three areas: metaethics, normative ethical theory, and applied ethics. Metaethics looks for possible foundations of ethics. Are there any moral facts out there from which we can deduce our moral theories? Normative ethical theories suggest principles or sets of principles to distinguish morally good from morally bad actions; whereas applied ethics looks at particular moral issues, such as, euthanasia or bribery.

However, this classification is not adequate to accommodate evolutionary ethics in its entirety. Instead, a different three-fold distinction of ethics seems appropriate: descriptive ethics, normative ethics, and metaethics. Descriptive ethics outlines ethical beliefs as held by various people and tries to explain why they are held. For instance, almost all human cultures believe that incest is morally wrong. This belief developed, it could be argued, because it provides a survival advantage to the group that entertains it. Normative ethical theories develop standards to judge which actions are good and which actions are bad. The standard as defended by evolutionary ethics would be something like "Actions that increase the long-term capacity of survival in evolutionary terms are good and actions that decrease this capacity are bad." However, the field has not yet established itself credibly in normative ethics. Consequentialism, deontology, virtue ethics, and social contracts still dominate debates. This is partly due to the excesses of Social Darwinism but also due to the unintuitive nature of the above or similar standards. Evolutionary ethics has been more successful in providing interesting answers in metaethics. Michael Ruse (1995 : 250), for instance, argues that morality is a "collective illusion of the genes, bringing us all in. We need to believe in morality, and so, thanks to our biology, we do believe in morality. There is no foundation 'out there' beyond human nature."

Descriptive ethics seems, as yet, the most interesting area for evolutionary ethics, a topic particularly suitable for anthropological and sociological research. Which ethical beliefs do people hold and why? But in all the three areas, challenges are to be faced.

**(iii) Challenges for Evolutionary Ethics**

The following are some lingering challenges for evolutionary ethics :

How can a trait that was developed under the pressure of natural selection explain moral actions that go far beyond reciprocal altruism or enlightened self-interest? How can, for instance, the action of Maximilian Kolbe be explained from a biological point of view? (Kolbe was a Polish priest who starved himself to death in a concentration camp to rescue a fellow prisoner.)

Could not human beings have moved beyond their biological roots and transcended their evolutionary origins, in which case, they would be able to formulate goals in the pursuit of goodness, beauty, and truth that "have nothing to do directly with survival, and which may, at times, militate against survival?" (O'Hear, 1997: 203)

Morality is universal, whereas biologically useful altruism is particular, favouring the family or the group over others. "Do not kill" does not only refer to one's own son, but also to the son of strangers. How can evolutionary ethics cope with universality?

Normative ethics aims to be action-guiding. How could humans ever judge an action to be ensuring long-term survival? (This is a practical rather than conceptual problem for evolutionary ethics.)

Hume's 'is/ought' problem still remains a challenge for evolutionary ethics. How can one move from 'is' (findings from the natural sciences, including, biology and sociobiology) to 'ought'?

Similarly, despite the length of time that has passed since the publication of *Principia Ethica*, the challenge of the 'naturalistic fallacy' remains.

Evolutionary ethics is, on a philosopher's time-scale, a very new approach to ethics. Though interdisciplinary approaches between scientists and philosophers have the potential to generate important new ideas, evolutionary ethics still has a long way to go.

## 1.3 Causes of Unethical Behaviour

Unethical behaviour can be caused by a number of reasons. Unethical behaviour is defined as *"behaviour that contradicts rules designed to maintain the fairness and morality of a situation"*. An example of unethical behaviour is a representative of a company taking kickbacks or bribes from a salesman for preferential treatment. Behaviour like this is motivated by various causes.

1. **Pressure:** Pressure to succeed, pressure to get ahead, pressure to meet deadlines and expectations, pressure from co-workers, bosses, customers, or vendors to engage in unethical activities or at least look the other way can be a big cause of unethical behaviour.

2. **Confusion:** Some people make unethical choices because they are not sure about what really is the right thing to do. Often, ethical problems are complicated, and the proper choice may be far from obvious.

3. **Personal Greed:** Self-interest, personal gain, ambition, and downright greed are at the causes of a lot of unethical activity in business.

4. **Misguided Loyalty:** It may be another cause of unethical conduct in a business or on a job. Many employees sometimes lie because they think they are being loyal to the organisation or to their employer. For example, managers at automobile companies who hide or falsify information about defects that later cause accidents and kill people or managers at pharmaceutical companies who hide information about dangerous side effects of their drugs.

5. **Lack of Personal Ethical Values:** Some people may have never learned or do not care about ethical values. Because they have no personal ethical values, they do not have any basis for understanding or applying ethical standards in business. These people do not think about right and wrong. They only think, "What's in it for me?" and "Can I get away with it?"

6. **Unrealistic Business Objectives:** Pressure to meet unrealistic business objectives and deadlines are the leading factors most likely to cause unethical behaviour.

7. **Environment:** Working in an environment with distrust or diminished morale, improper training about, or ignorance that, acts are unethical; and the lack of consequences when caught are the next leading factors likely to cause unethical behaviour.

## Points to Remember

- **Ethics** is concerned not only with distinguishing right from wrong and good from bad but also with commitment to do what is right or what is good.
- **Morals** and **morality** are about personal behaviour. Morals are principles or habits with respect to right or wrong conduct. It defines how things should work according to an individuals' ideals and principles.
- There are many **types of ethics**, such as:
  1. Normative Ethic
  2. Meta-Ethics
  3. Descriptive Ethics

4. Relational Ethics
   5. Applied Ethics
   6. Evolutionary Ethics

- **Normative ethics** involves arriving at moral standards that regulate right and wrong conduct. In a sense, it is a search for an ideal test of proper behaviour.
- **Metaethics** can be defined as the study of the origin and meaning of ethical concepts.
- **Descriptive ethics** is sometimes referred to as comparative ethics because so much activity can involve comparing ethical systems: comparing the ethics of the past to the present, comparing the ethics of one society to another and comparing the ethics which people claim to follow with the actual rules of conduct which do describe their actions.
- **Relativism** is the position that all points of view are equally valid and the individual determines what is true and relative for them. Relativism theorises that truth is different for different people, not simply that different people believe different things to be true.
- **Applied ethics** is the branch of ethics which consists of the analysis of specific, controversial moral issues, such as, abortion, animal rights, or euthanasia.
- **Evolutionary ethics** tries to bridge the gap between philosophy and the natural sciences by arguing that natural selection has instilled human beings with a moral sense, a disposition to be good.
- **Unethical behaviour can be caused** by a number of reasons.
   1. Pressure
   2. Confusion
   3. Personal Greed
   4. Misguided loyalty
   5. Lack of personal ethical values
   6. Pressure to meet unrealistic business objectives and deadlines
   7. Environment

## Questions for Discussion

1. What is ethics? Explain with definitions.
2. Explain the term "morality". What relationship exists between morality and ethics?
3. Explain the nature and importance of ethics.
4. What are the different types of ethics? Explain.
5. Define the term business ethics.
6. Discuss the nature and importance of business ethics.
7. Examine the causes of unethical behaviour.

# Chapter 2...
# Areas of Business Ethics

## Contents ...

2.1 Introduction
2.2 Meaning, Nature and Importance of Business Ethics
    2.2.1 Meaning of Business Ethics
    2.2.2 Nature of Business Ethics
    2.2.3 Importance of Business Ethics
2.3 Types of Business Ethics
2.4 Factors Influencing Business Ethics
2.5 Corporate Ethics – Ethical Behaviour and Audit of Ethical Behaviour
    2.5.1 Evaluation of Corporate Codes
    2.5.2 Formal Committee and Audit System
    2.5.3 Environmental Auditing
    2.5.4 Organisational Auditing
    2.5.5 The Relevance of Ethical Audit
    2.5.6 The Model of an Ethical Audit
2.6 Individual Ethics
    2.6.1 Aspects in Individual Ethics
    2.6.2 Individual Ethical Decision-making
    2.6.3 Factors Affecting Ethical Decision-making
2.7 Professional Ethics
    2.7.1 Professions and Professionalism
    2.7.2 Professional Ethical Codes
    2.7.3 Analysis of a Professional Ethical Code
    2.7.4 Characteristics of a Professional Ethical Code
2.8 Gandhian Philosophy of Ethical Behaviour
2.9 Social Audit
- Points to Remember
- Questions for Discussion

# Business Ethics

**Learning Objectives ...**
- To be aware of the ten commandments of ethical behaviour
- To study the Gandhian philosophy of ethical behaviour
- To be able to differentiate between individual and professional ethics
- To explore corporate ethics and learn about the concept of social audit

## 2.1 Introduction

Business ethics is nothing but the application of ethics in business. Business ethics is the application of general ethical ideas to business behaviour. Ethical business behaviour facilitates and promotes good to society, improves profitability, fosters business relations and employee productivity. The concept of business ethics has come to mean various things to various people, but generally it's coming to know what it right or wrong in the workplace and doing what's right - this is in regard to effects of products/ services and in relationships with stakeholders.

## 2.2 Meaning, Nature and Importance of Business Ethics

### 2.2.1 Meaning of Business Ethics

Business ethics is concerned with the behaviour of a businessman in doing a business. Unethical practices are creating problems to businessman and business units. The life and growth of a business unit depends upon the ethics practiced by a businessman. Business ethics are developed by the passage of time and custom. A custom differs from one business to another. If a custom is adopted and accepted by businessman and public, that custom will become an ethic. Business ethics is applicable to every type of business. The social responsibility of a business requires the observing of business ethics. A business man should not ignore business ethics while assuming social responsibility. Business ethics means the behaviour of a businessman while conducting a business, by observing morality in his business activities.

- According to **Wheeler**, *"Business Ethics is an art and science for maintaining harmonious relationship with society, its various groups and institutions as well as reorganising the moral responsibility for the rightness and wrongness of business conduct."*
- According to **Rogene. A. Buchholz**, *"Business ethics refers to right or wrong behaviour in business decisions".*
- According to **Cater Mcnamara**, *"Business ethics is generally coming to know what is right or wrong in the workplace and doing what is right- this is in regard to effects of products/services and in relationship with stake holders."*

- *"Business Ethics attempts to apply general moral principles to business activities in order to resolve, or at least clarify, the moral issues which typically arise in business".*

  **Elizebeth Vallance,**

- *"Business Ethics is the process of evaluating decions, either pre or post, with respect to the moral standards of the society's culture".*

  **David J. Fitzsche**

- *"Business Ethics is the study of how personal moral norms apply to the activities and goals of commercial enterprise. It is not a separate moral standard, but the study of how the business context poses its own unique problems for the moral person who acts as an agent of this system".*

Aristotle defined 'virtue' as a matter of habit or the trained faculty of choice. Business Ethics reflects the habits and choices managers make concerning their own activities and those of the rest of the organisation".

> "The way in which the choices are framed, analysed, and either maintained or abandoned form the basic objective of the Business Ethics inquiry. The validation of Business Ethics, however, unpopular as a term, is simply a way of acknowledging that indeed, there are choices to be made concerning the means and ends which have essentially moral ingredients".

**(Laura L. Nash, Good Intentions Aside – P. 5 - 6)**

## 2.2.2 Nature of Business Ethics

1. **Provides Basic Framework:** Business ethics provides the framework within which business is to be conducted. It suggests cultural, social, legal, moral, and economic limits within which business has to be operated. Ethics suggests what is good and what is bad in business.
2. **Code of Conduct:** Business ethics is the code of conduct which businessmen should follow while conducting their normal business activities.
3. **Based on Moral and Social Values:** Business ethics is based on well-accepted moral/principal values. It recommends moral of conduct for businessmen. It includes fair treatment to social groups, service to society and self-control.
4. **Needs Willing Acceptance for Enforcement:** Business ethics cannot be enforced by law or by force. It must be accepted by businessmen as self-discipline. It should come from within.
5. **Education and Guidance Required for Introduction:** Businessman should be given proper education, training and guidance to motivate them for following ethical business practices.

6. **Not Against Profit Making:** Business Ethics is not against fair profit making. However, it is against making profit by cheating and exploiting consumers, employees or investors. It supports expansion of business but by fair means and not through corrupt practices or illegal activities.

### 2.2.3 Importance of Business Ethics

1. **Survival of Business:** Business ethics are mandatory for the survival of any business. Businesses with unethical practices may have short-term success, but they will fail in the long run. This is because a consumer can be cheated only once. After that, the consumer will not buy goods from that businessman. He will also inform others not to buy from that businessman. So this will defame his image and creates negative publicity. This will result in failure of the business. Therefore, if the businessmen do not follow ethical rules, he will fail in the market. So, it is always better for a businessman to follow appropriate code of conduct to survive in the market.

2. **Smooth Functioning:** If the business follows all the ethical norms, then the employees, shareholders, consumers, dealers and suppliers will all be happy. And the business will get full cooperation from them. This will result in smooth functioning of the business. So, the business will grow, expand and diversify easily and quickly. It will have higher sales and higher profits.

3. **Safeguarding Consumers' Rights:** The consumer has many rights such as right to be informed, right to choose, right to health and safety, right to be heard, right to redress, etc. But many businessmen do not respect and protect these rights. Ethical practices are essential to safeguard these rights of the consumers.

4. **Improve Customers' Confidence:** Ethical practices helps in improving the customers' confidence about the quality, quantity, price, etc. of the products. The customers have more trust and confidence in the businessmen who follow ethical rules. They feel that such businessmen will not cheat them.

5. **Develops Good Relations:** Business ethics helps in developing good and friendly relations between business and society. It will result in a regular supply of good quality products and services at low prices to the society. It will also result in profits for the businesses thereby resulting in growth of economy.

6. **Consumer Satisfaction:** In present scenario, the consumer is the king of the market. Any business simply cannot survive without the consumers. Therefore, the main aim of business is consumer satisfaction. Dissatisfaction on the part of consumers will lead to no sales and thus no profits too. Consumer will be satisfied only if the business follows all the business ethics, and hence are highly needed.

7. **Protecting Stakeholders:** Business ethics are required to protect the interest of all the stakeholders, i.e., employees, shareholders, competitors, dealers, suppliers, etc. It protects them from exploitation through unfair trade practices.

8. **Creates Good Image:** Business ethics create a good image for the business and businessmen. If the businessmen follow all ethical rules, then they will be fully accepted and not criticised by the society.
9. **Consumer Movement:** Business ethics are gaining more and more importance because of the growth of the consumer movement. Today, the consumers are aware of their rights. Now they are more organised and hence cannot be cheated easily. They take actions against those businessmen who indulge in bad business practices. They boycott poor quality, harmful, high-priced and counterfeit (duplicate) goods. Therefore, the only way to survive in business is to be honest and fair.
10. **Importance of Labour:** Labour plays a crucial role in the success of any business. Therefore, while dealing with them, businessmen must use business ethics. They must be given proper wages and salaries and provided with better working conditions. There must be good relations between employer and employees. The employees must also be given proper welfare facilities.
11. **Healthy Competition:** The business must use code of conduct while dealing with the competitors. There must be healthy competition among the competitors. Cut-throat competition should not exist. Similarly, equal opportunities to small-scale business should be given. Monopoly must be avoided. This is because a monopoly is harmful to the consumers.
12. **Stop Business Malpractices:** Some businessmen gets involved in business malpractices by indulging in unfair trade practices like adulteration, cheating in weights and measures, artificial high pricing, black-marketing, selling of duplicate and harmful products, hoarding, etc. These business malpractices are harmful to the consumers. Business ethics help to stop these business malpractices.

## 2.3 Types of Business Ethics

Business ethics is basically a type of principle of applied ethics, which analyses various ethical rules and ethical or moral problems that may take place in a commercial environment.

In the twenty-first century, one of the most significant aspects of the commercial marketplaces all over the world is the growing focus on conscience. As a result, the necessity for highly ethical business practices (which is also referred as ethicism) is on the rise. At the same time, force is also being applied on businesses and industries for the development of business ethics with the help of novel public efforts and regulations (for example, increased amount of road tax in the United Kingdom for vehicles with higher emission

Business ethics can take the form of a descriptive field (subject area) or normative field. The descriptive discipline is applied in the academic world. The normative discipline is basically implemented as a corporate device and it is also utilised in the form of career specialisation.

The number and degree of business ethical issues gives the evidence of how much a business is compliant with the social values (non-economic).

There are three important types of ethics, namely, transactional ethics, participatory ethics and recognition ethics.

**1. Transactional Ethics :** Man is a social animal. He has to act and react with others through different transactions. The practice of ethics in all these transactions is called as transactional ethics. All involved parties should reciprocate ethical practices. The common good ethical interests are binding all the people. It is a win-win approach from all prospective.

Let us take the example of a medical doctor. He examines the patients, gives the right type of treatment and charges moderately. The patients are also reciprocating on getting the treatment from this doctor and promote a word-of-mouth communication. The principle of honesty is the basic principle in transactional ethics. The interest of both the parties is taken care of.

**2. Participatory Ethics:** It is an important part of business ethics. Guided by common good, all the participants follow some ethical practices. The important features of participatory ethics are:

(a) All the parties like consumers, producers and employees maintain some basic ethical standards.

(b) The level of participation depends on the degree of motivation in the society.

(c) Participation comes from external forces and inner commitment. This can take place only through the process of creating ethical awareness.

(d) The level of participation has to be watched by all the groups leading to mutual checks and balances.

Special attention has to be given to the least powerful and marginalised sections of society.

(e) The growth of participation indicates the level of social development. It is the growth of solidarity in an angle of individualism. Many social-economic problems of developed countries are solved by the ethical practices.

**3. Recognition Ethics**: As human beings, people are endowed with the ability to understand the problems of others. This quality leads to the recognition of individuals, institutions and societies, conflicting situations can be solved by the correct recognition of the situation. This requires a correct perspective and empathy. The strong is helping the weak. The learned is helping the lesser learned. The experienced is helping the new entrant. Compensation is given to victims.

## 2.4 Factors Influencing Business Ethics

Though there are many factors which affect Business Ethics, a few are mentioned below:

**1. Behaviour: Personal Code of Conduct**

As we know, the boundaries of legally acceptable behaviour are wider than those of Ethical Behaviour. A person's behaviour may be legally correct however it may not necessarily be ethically appropriate.

- a) **Disclosing commercial details of a competitor to a potential customer:** While this is quite rampant in the business world, it is not ethical.

- b) **Inappropriate Computer Use:** Employees may use company computers to engage in unethical behaviour. For example, an employee who is not permitted to use the Internet for personal reasons commits an unethical act by shopping online while at work. Random Internet surfing takes away from the time he/ she spend on work-related activities. Employees sometimes use company email to spread inappropriate websites or videos to co-workers, some of which could be deemed offensive by the recipients.

- c) **Time Misuse:** Unethical behaviour can include stealing time from the company, as the company is compensating employees and receiving no productivity in return. In addition to time spent on aimless Internet surfing, time misuse can consist of extending breaks beyond the allotted time, congregating around the water cooler or engaging in lengthy gossip sessions during working time, falsifying time sheets, coming into work late or leaving early and running personal errands while travelling on company business.

- d) **Sexual Harassment and Bullying:** An employee could commit unethical behaviour by sexually harassing co-workers. This could involve making lewd comments, touching inappropriately or making unwanted sexual advances.

  Bullying typically involves attempting to intimidate a co-worker by making demeaning comments about him, spreading gossip or even making verbal or physical threats. In general, a bully attempts to make the workplace as uncomfortable as possible for a co-worker. In some cases, ongoing bullying can escalate into violence in the workplace.

- e) **Illegal Acts:** Some unethical acts can also be illegal. For example, an employee who has access to a company's financial records, such as a bookkeeper or accountant, could use his/her access and expertise to misuse company funds. An HR representative could commit identity theft or sell personal data to other companies.

**2. Policies & Framework**

Organisational policies and available framework to deal with ethical issues / cases affect ethical behaviour of an employee. The policies and framework decide how committed a company is to implement ethical practices.

**Policies mean:**
   (a) Listing down what is ethical behaviour and what is unethical behaviour
   (b) Enforcing upon employees to comply with the expected behaviour.
   (c) Linking their performance appraisal / confirmation / survival in the company with their ethical behaviour.

**Framework necessarily means:**

**(a) Ombudsman process in case of a situation :**

e.g. large IT companies and a few business houses (such as Tata Sons, Wipro, Infosys) are particular about their employees adhering to the Policies & Framework available. Wipro has a COBC Certification course, which is mandatory for every employee to pass. Secondly Wipro has Ombudsman in place and employees undergo routine training on ethical & unethical cases which have happened in recent times.

**(b) Fair Trial (Unethical behaviour) :**

In case an employee crosses the boundaries of ethical behaviour, he/she should be provided with a fair trial. Wipro's Ombudsman process provides the accused and victim fair chance to put forth his/her point.

**3. Ethical Standards of Top Management**

Employees follow Top Management's behaviour without expressing. If the Chief of the company behaves unethically ill-treats his female colleagues, misuses company funds, then the employees are more likely to be unethical & corrupt.

e.g. Many examples can be cited.... Satyam Computers' CEO Ramalinga Raju's behaviour was a classical case. Enron's CEO and Chairman were at the peak of unethical practices which led Enron down the drain.

**4. Ethical climate of the country**

Actually Ethical Climate of the company is resultant of the above 3 parameters. Nevertheless, Ethical Climate is essential for the company's survival and growth in an ethical manner. Companies may have ethical people at top leading the company in right direction, it may also have Policies & Framework in place at the same time it may also have ethical employees... even after this, the company may get caught in the web of unethical business practices. Climate also gets affected by the Financial Reward system of the company. If company is able to investigate and pick out unethical behaviour and punish accordingly it passes a strong message to its employees. Similarly if the company rewards ethical behaviour regardless of the amount of commercial success this behaviour has brought, it creates ethical climate and encourages people to behave ethically.

e.g. Many examples can be cited again here. Let's look at Coca Cola India and Pespsico India... while it's not clear whether the top management was involved in the pesticide case or not, the climate definitely was not promoting ethical practices.

Other examples could be: Dow Chemicals in Dehu Road, Union Carbide's Bhopal Gas Tragedy and post gas leak. Everything points to the ethical climate of a company.

## 2.5 Corporate Ethics-Ethical Behaviour and Audit of Ethical Behaviour

Corporate ethics are relevant to all aspects of business conduct, including board strategies, how companies treat employees and suppliers, sales and marketing techniques and accounting practices.

Corporate ethics go beyond the legal requirements for businesses and concerns optional decisions and behaviour guided by values. Therefore, ethics in the business world are relevant both to the conduct of individuals and the conduct of the organisation as a whole.

Corporate, business and organisational ethics are terms that can be used interchangeably. According to O. C. Ferrel, *"Organisational or corporate ethics is one of the most important and yet the most overlooked and misunderstood of concepts in business ethics"*. Usually, it is associated with the core values espoused by a given corporate or organisation. These core values are commonly written up in a code of conduct, which serves as a central guide for the day-to-day decision-making within the organisation in question.

The proper understanding of corporate ethics is essential for developing ethical leadership. This is so, since organisations want to be seen as good corporate citizens, whose behaviour and dealings are both ethical and fair. There are a number of benefits for organisations that adhere to sound ethical values, including an enhancement of executive standards of behaviour, i.e., the "tone at the top," the positive motivation of employees, the protection of the given organisation's reputation, the fostering of greater respect for laws and regulations, and improved business relationships.

"Corporate or organisational ethics" refers to the generally accepted standards that guide behaviour in business and other organisational contexts. Business ethics in the corporate area require values-based leadership from top management, purposeful actions that include, planning and implementation of standards of appropriate conduct, as well as openness and continuous effort to improve the organisation's ethical performance. Although personal values are important in ethical decision-making, they are just one of the components that guide the decisions, actions, and policies of all organisations.

The burden of ethical behaviour relates to the organisation's values and traditions, not just to the individuals who make the decisions and carry them out. A firm's ability to plan and implement ethical business standards depends in part on structuring resources and activities to achieve ethical objectives in an effective and efficient manner.

Corporate ethics apply to all aspects of business conduct, including board strategies, how companies treat employees and suppliers, sales and marketing techniques and accounting practices.

The Cadbury Committee made a strong recommendation that it should be regarded as good practice for board of directors to draw up **codes of ethics or statements of business practice** and to publish them both internally and externally. This was the culmination of interest in ethical codes and belief in their central importance for achieving the business aim as was developing in the USA and Europe. The larger companies in the Fortune 500 or the FTSE 100 – being seen as elite groups, showed the way. The awareness of the importance of publicly declared ethical commitments is a part of the spirit of the times, the **Zeitgeist**, and these have become internalised. This has demonstrated the fact that the need of the hour is to constantly audit the relationship between the publicly professed theory and their practice which is carried out publicly, as well as in private.

Although most corporations, these days, have their corporate code in place, they still are not moral codes. This is so, since no one – whether individual or group – can make actions moral by fiat. Thus, every code has to be evaluated specifically for its ethicality. Some codes specify the legal requirements, and some make mention of specific concerns, such as, bribery or illegal political contributions, which employees ought to know. Some others mention practices and procedures that may cause conflict of interest. Even industry-wise codes seeking to set standards of fair competition have a limitation. They cannot, for instance, restrict trade or competition, by price-fixing, and standardisation of the hours of work.

### 2.5.1 Evaluation of Corporate Codes

Many of these corporate codes suffer from many shortcomings, on closer analysis. They do not reveal the basis of the codes, in the sense that - how the codes were formed, what moral principles are sought to be implemented or, how to resolve issues of interpretation or of conflicts not covered by the code. To be moral means to know the 'whys' of the tasks, besides obeying someone's 'right' orders. When faced with a serious moral dilemma, how can the code help a member of a firm or profession determine the course of his action? Seeking the help of the legal office (as the codes usually direct) will only give us the legal view, but not solve the moral dilemma. Unless the code is understood in terms of its moral principles, the people would feel that they should be learnt by rote, or, that they are impossible ideals never meant to be attained in the first place.

The codes would be beneficial only when the workers understand how the rules are derived, and how they could implement the moral principles. Ideally, each member should not only understand its moral principles but also the nature of his profession or firm. He would then be able to derive the same code clearly and objectively, when faced with the moral issues dealt with specifically by the corporate code.

The corporate codes may have limited usefulness. Yet, it cannot be said that they serve a very useful purpose. Firstly, the very exercise of developing a corporate code forces all the people concerned to think through their corporate mission in a fresh way and sort out the obligations individually and as a corporate body towards their customers, employees, clients and societies as a whole.

The code, on being made public, will generate continuing discussion and further refinement of the code. New employees would absorb the perspective of responsibility and the need to think and act morally. The employees could use the code as a guide and touchstone of action when confronted with immoral orders. Lastly, the code will assure both customers and the public of the fact that the firm adheres to moral principles, and provides them with a criterion for evaluating the firm's action morally.

### 2.5.2 Formal Committee and Audit System

*An audit is a well-known procedure to ensure that a company's financial and accounting systems 'are providing accurate and up-to-date information on its current financial position' and also that it's published 'financial statements represent a true and fair reflection of this position'* (Quoted in "A framework for Internal Control" Chartered Institute of Management Accountants 1922 p. 1). Its importance cannot be emphasised more. Its interactive nature has been a vital check on the financial aspect, but in addition, it can pinpoint the failures of the past so that they can act as the warnings of the present and the future practices.

A recent innovation has been made to create an ethical auditing process. At first sight, it might look impossible, for ethics is qualitative and therefore not quantifiable. Values cannot be weighed or empirically tested. But audits have moved on to new areas like, the environmental and organisational fields, in addition to their financial role. The auditing of ethical acts may not be as straightforward and streamlined as others, but not beyond the scope of practicability.

The extension of audit beyond financial auditing is already well established in North America and also in large European concerns, and is, of late, getting a toehold in the UK. Initially, it covered issues like compliance with laws and regulations, and insurance. It is also asked to review the business procedures and comment on their adequacy. The environmental laws have been largely expanded by legislation, and compliance with them is yet another requirement being examined by audit.

### 2.5.3 Environmental Auditing

Environmental auditing uses a systematic approach to every aspect of manufacturing, office and field safety procedures to find out their effect on the environment and suggest ways and means to minimise their adverse effects. It forces positive change. Such specific areas may call for policy modifications or systematic structural changes. For example, a manufacturing industry may have a different impact on the environment as compared to a service industry.

It would therefore be necessary to evaluate the adverse impacts on environment, at every stage, right from the sourcing of raw materials to the final consumption by the end-user, through manufacturing, packaging, transport, distribution, and reshipment. Also, the disposal of waste needs to be audited at every stage. Product safety falls under the head.

### 2.5.4 Organisational Auditing

Today, many businesses have introduced this procedure with the objective of identifying improvements in the operation and delivery of their service wherein the given corporation initiates the audit by first setting the standards of operation. Thereafter, it is closely monitored. The process of auditing invariably involves a survey of the operation. In the light of the findings, the standards are modified and developed, accordingly. Then, monitoring of the modified procedures and effects is carried out constantly.

With the help of the feedback obtained from further auditing, appropriate changes are effected leading to improved performance. This is a continuous iterative process. This process is more dialectical than circular, as the audit findings are used to improve business practice, which is then pursued at a new higher level of awareness, in terms of more rigorous and more focused targets and standards.

### 2.5.5 The Relevance of Ethical Audit

The process of auditing financial, environmental and more recently organisational arrangements have been found to be both informative and useful. But the question remains as to whether the auditing of values is a practical issue. If business ethics can make a difference, then, it should be possible and even necessary to identify what that difference is and to what extent it has made the difference.

A device has to be designed to identify the factors and their exact role in the given organisation. Otherwise, the benefits of such an exercise like ethical auditing will be too valuable to be ignored. They are mainly on these lines: Auditing will make business articulate its ethical priorities. Second, it will make explicit the successes and shortcomings of business. Thirdly, the feedback provided will ensure a healthy process of continuous improvement.

### 2.5.6 The Model of an Ethical Audit

To begin with, an audit opens with the value statements and policies of the business. It points the extent to which structures and systems within the business support these values or fail to do so. It becomes crucial to implement the ethical strategy just as they do in the case of the financial strategy.

The systems and structures are to be so refashioned (if need be) that making a ethical and, therefore, the right thing becomes an easy and natural way of the work ethos of the firm concerned. For doing so, the audit has to bring to light those areas which impede the implementation of values. In short, this amounts to constantly auditing the relationship between theory and practice.

More specifically, these would be looked into: Is the policy statement clearly worded? Has the value statement been made with the inputs of all the vital sectors of the firm, and have contributions been obtained from people at all levels? Communication is the next topic of interest: Is the code well-publicised internally and externally, so that it is accessible to everyone that matters? Is there a clear and overt leadership thrust from the top in applying the stated values throughout the business?

The audit will investigate into product and service standard, regarding their quality, reliability, repute; this is done from the viewpoint of all the stakeholders. More significantly, the questions asked frequently would be these: Are their mechanisms in place to constantly monitor quality, and to deal with problems related to quality? Also, does everyone connected with this area know the existence of such mechanisms in place?

The appropriateness of management structures along with the lines of accountability and responsibility as also the constitutional arrangements of the business are the next line of auditing. Is their proper communication internally and externally with other stakeholders? Human resource development is the next line of approach. Does business value people, in general, and more particularly, its own people? Are their clear and ethical policies set out and practised in hiring, grading, promoting, selecting, and reducing the work-force? Are there satisfactory channels and procedures for employee appeals, grievances, disputes and appeals?

Concrete and specific answers to such questions elicited and monitored constantly will prove the ethical state of business and reveal the extent of justice and decency, the basic human values enshrined in the organisation concerned.

In conclusion, formal committees' audits are a way of bringing together theory and practice. They reveal how far the business is permeated with ethical principles and what further reforms are needed. They are a crucial element in the reiterative process which can ensure that an organisation is ethical and remains so for as long as business prospers.

## 2.6 Individual Ethics

Individual ethics are the generally accepted principles of right and wrong governing the conduct of individuals. Individual or personal ethics are the moral foundation on which people build their lives. They assist in decision-making, guiding an individual to participate in actions that meet his/her internal moral standards.

Ethics represents the core value system one uses for everyday problem solving. They create a framework for determining 'right' versus 'wrong'. Ethics are developed throughout life based on a wide variety of factors. They are not absolute rules. For many people, to define personal ethics is a difficult endeavour. They simply consider their 'inner voice' to be all the ethical guidance they need. For most of us, intuition plays a large role in what one finds ethical.

In today's world, the individuals concerned can make a single decision that can have a profoundly positive or negative effect on their family, their employer, co-workers, a nation, and even on the entire world. The life we lead reflects the strength of a single trait: our personal character. Personal ethics are different for each person but for the most part, people want to be known as a good person, someone who can be trusted, and he or she are concerned about his or her relationships and personal reputation.

### 2.6.1 Aspects in Individual Ethics

When defining personal ethics, there are several aspects to consider which can vary greatly from person to person. To put it in analytical terms, personal ethics impact behaviours which generally fall into the following framework:

1. **Value of Others:** Ethics relates considerably to how one person treats another person in terms of respect, concern for their well-being and recognition of their autonomy. It strongly impacts the depth and longevity of relationships.
2. **Value of Society:** How one interacts with society as a whole also speaks of their ethical standards. This includes compliance with the law, conforming to generally accepted social norms, and contributing to the community.
3. **Value of Self:** How a person presents themselves is an indicator of personal ethics. This refers to trustworthiness, honesty, reliability, and consistency.

In other words, you can see the physical manifestation of your personal ethics in decisions and behaviours that impact your relationships with others, your role in society and your personal identity. Though this framework is not necessarily comprehensive, it provides a basic platform on which to evaluate the role of ethics in everyday life.

In discussing business ethics, one must discuss personal ethics and the question of individual motivation vs. professional conduct. It is an interesting distinction. In personal motivation, we can often make the ends justify the means and as long as the means do not violate any laws, we can feel that it is appropriate. In business ethics, it is often the conduct that should be the prime concern. Corporate entities in themselves are neutral, they have no motivations or ulterior motives, it is the people those who occupy key positions in management that matters. A corporate charter and a company policy are in place to circumvent any individual motives and create a code of conduct while at work or representing the agency.

One approach to understanding organisational ethics is to take an individual perspective and focus on personal morals, character and the person. This approach assumes that virtues linked to the high moral ground of truthfulness, honesty, and fairness is self-evident and easy to apply in a complex global environment. This approach would assume that organisational values and ethics training may be more appropriate for individuals with unacceptable moral development. It also assumes that employees will be able to control their decision-making environment independent of managers and co-workers. Another approach to understanding business ethics is to assume that organisational values and compliance systems are necessary to prevent people from engaging in unethical conduct. This approach recognises the risks and the complex decision-making in a global environment.

Business ethics programmes and organisations combine values and compliance, which requires training and constant vigilance. All organisations will face ethical lapses, unintentional misconduct, and complacency from employees when they observe serious misconduct.

Business ethics programmes and organisations combine values and compliance, which requires training and constant vigilance. All organisations will face ethical lapses, unintentional misconduct, and complacency from employees when they observe serious misconduct.

The scandals and unethical conduct that have occurred globally have taught us that some people deliberately break the law or engage in improper behaviour. Many others never see ethical issues when devising what they think as an innovative scheme for success. In the U.S., the Supreme Court and the Federal Sentencing Guidelines for Organisations (FSGO) hold organisations responsible for the conduct of their employees, most firms have decided to implement ethics and compliance programmes to prevent misconduct and diminish the risk associated with employee wrongdoing. The 2004 Amendments to the FSGO hold the governing authority, usually the board of directors, responsible for ethical leadership including an effective ethics programme and internal ethics audits. In addition, an ethics officer with adequate resources is required to report directly to the board or a committee of the board. Even though the majority of employees want to do the right thing, many people do not know the exact nature of the law and are totally surprised when they are charged with violations that were never anticipated. The legal system and the nature of civil litigation make ethical decision-making a 'mine field' for possible error without adequate knowledge of the potential risk of a decision.

The managers need to understand how ethical decisions are made and the environment that influences ethical decision-making. They face the same business ethics risks as others but managers should be more aware of those special risks associated with customer contact and interaction with their relevant stakeholders. While there may be many significant and meaningful aspects of ethics that can be taught to employees that will help them live a better life, there should be some foundational concepts taught to business employees that will help them obtain a holistic understanding of business ethics.

Many managers have a difficult time understanding that ethics requires going beyond minimal legal requirements. They find it a Herculean task insofar as evolving a framework that would help managers see the benefits of conducting oneself in accordance with the highest ethical standards. The best opportunity for achieving this goal would be an understanding of stakeholders that shape and form ethical issues and evaluations, and a description of how leadership, corporate culture, formal ethics programmes, and individual character are important to ethical decision-making.

Ethical decisions in the workplace are guided by the organisation's culture and the influence of others, such as co-workers, superiors, subordinates. In fact, more ethical misconduct is done to benefit organisational performance rather than to satisfy personal greed.

The ethical climate of an organisation is a significant element of organisational culture; whereas a firm's overall culture establishes ideals that guide a wide range of behaviours for members of the organisation, its ethical climate focuses specifically on issues of right and wrong.

The ethical climate is the organisation's character or conscience. The codes of conduct and ethics policies, top management's actions on ethical issues, the values and moral development and philosophies of co-workers, and the opportunity for misconduct all contribute to an organisation's ethical climate. In fact, the ethical climate actually determines whether or not certain dilemmas are perceived as having an ethical intensity level that requires a decision.

The organisations concerned can manage their culture and ethical climate by trying to hire employees whose values match their own. Some firms even measure potential employees' values during the hiring process and strive to choose individuals who 'fit' within the ethical climate rather than those whose beliefs and values differ significantly. A poor 'fit' can have very expensive ramifications for both organisations and employees. Beyond the potential for misconduct, a poor employee-organisation ethical fit usually results in low job satisfaction, decreased performance, and higher turnover (Sims and Kroeck, 1994).

Together, the organisational culture and the influence of co-workers may foster conditions that limit or permit misconduct. When these conditions provide rewards, such as, financial gain, recognition, promotion, or simply the good feeling from a job well done – the opportunity for unethical conduct may be encouraged, or discouraged, based on ethical climate. For example, a company policy that does not provide for punishment of employees who violate a rule insofar as not accepting large gifts from client provides an opportunity for unethical behaviour. Essentially, this lack of policy allows individuals to engage in such behaviour without fear of consequences. Thus, organisational policies, processes, and other factors may contribute to the opportunity to act unethically.

An opportunity usually relates to employees' immediate job context – where they work, with whom they work, and the nature of the work. The specific work situation includes the motivational 'carrots and sticks' that superiors can use to influence employee behaviour. Pay raises, bonuses, and public recognition constitute carrots, or positive reinforcement; whereas reprimands, pay penalties, demotions, and even firings act as sticks, the negative reinforcement. For example, a salesperson who is publicly recognised and given a large bonus for making a valuable sale that he obtained through unethical tactics will probably be motivated to use unethical sales tactics in the future, even if such behaviour goes against his personal value system.

Research has shown that there is a general tendency to discipline top sales performers more leniently than poor sales performers for engaging in identical forms of unethical selling behaviour (Bellizzi and Hasty, 2003). Neither a company policy stating that the behaviour in question was unacceptable nor a repeated pattern of unethical behaviour offset the general tendency to favour the top sales performers. A superior sales record appears to induce more lenient forms of discipline despite managerial actions that are specifically instituted to produce more equal forms of discipline. Based on their research, Bellizzi and Hasty concluded that an opportunity exists for top sales performers to be more unethical than poor sales performers.

This framework helps managers put ethical decision-making in organisational context and see how the process fits together. Once one begins to understand that good ethics is linked to organisational performance, they see why it is necessary to have organisational ethics and compliance programmes. Also, the managers begin to see the personal costs including reputation damage that arise from misconduct.

Is it possible for an individual with strong moral values to make ethically questionable decisions in a business setting? What affects a person's inclination to make either ethical or unethical decisions in a business organisation? Although the answers to that question are not entirely clear, there appears to be three general sets of factors that influence the standards of behaviour in an organisation; individual factors, social factors and opportunity.

Several individual factors influence the level of ethical behaviour in an organisation. An individual's knowledge level regarding an issue can help determine ethical behaviour. A decision-maker with a greater amount of knowledge regarding an object or situation may take steps to avoid ethical problems; whereas a less-informed person may unknowingly take action that leads to an ethical conflict. One's moral values and central value-related attitudes clearly influence his or her business behaviour. Most people join organisations to accomplish personal goals. The types of personal goals an individual aspires to and the manner in which these goals are pursued have significant impact on that individual's behaviour in an organisation.

A person's behaviour in the workplace is, to some degree, determined by cultural norms, and these social factors vary from one culture to another. For example, in some countries, it is acceptable and ethical for customs agents to receive gratuities for performing ordinary legal tasks that are a part of jobs; whereas in other countries, these practices would be viewed as unethical and perhaps illegal. The actions and decisions of co-workers is another social factor believed to shape a person's sense of business ethics. For example, if your co-workers make long-distance telephone calls on company time and at company expense, you might view that behaviour as acceptable and ethical because everyone does it. Significant others are persons to whom someone is emotionally attached - spouses, friends, and relatives, for instance. Their moral values and attitudes can also affect an employee's perception of what is ethical or otherwise in the workplace.

By opportunity is meant the amount of freedom an organisation gives an employee to behave ethically if he or she makes that choice. In some organisations, certain company policies and procedures reduce the opportunity to be unethical. For example, at some fast food restaurants, one person takes your order and receives your payment and another person fills the order. This procedure reduces the opportunity to be unethical because the person handling the money is not dispensing the product, and the person giving out the product is not handling the money. The existence of an ethical code and the importance management places on this code are other determinants of opportunity. The degree of enforcement of company policies, procedures, and ethical codes is a major force affecting opportunity. When violations are dealt with consistently and firmly, the opportunity to be unethical is reduced considerably.

## 2.6.2 Individual Ethical Decision-making

There are many approaches to the individual ethical decision-making process in business. However, one of the more common approaches was developed by James Rest and has been called the four-step or four-stage model of individual ethical decision-making. Numerous scholars have applied this theory in the business context. The four steps include: ethical issue recognition, ethical (moral) judgement, ethical (moral) intent, and ethical (moral) behaviour.

1. **Ethical Issue Recognition:** Before a person can apply any standards of ethical philosophy to an issue, he or she must first comprehend that the issue has an ethical component. This means that the ethical decision-making process must be 'triggered' or set in motion by the awareness of an ethical dilemma. Some individuals are likely to be more sensitive to potential ethical problems than others. A plethora of factors can affect whether or not someone recognises an ethical issue.

2. **Ethical (Moral) Judgement:** If an individual is confronted with a situation or issue that he or she recognises as having an ethical component or posing an ethical dilemma, the individual will probably form some overall impression or judgment about the rightness or wrongness of the issue. The individual may reach this judgment in a variety of ways, as noted in the earlier section on ethical philosophy.

3. **Ethical (Moral) Intent:** Once an individual reaches an ethical judgment about a situation or issue, the next stage in the decision-making process is to form a behavioural intent. That is, the individual decides what he or she will do (or not do) in regard to the perceived ethical dilemma.

According to research, ethical judgments are a strong predictor of behavioural intent. However, individuals do not always form intentions to behave that are in accord with their judgments, as various situational factors may act to influence the individual otherwise.

4. **Ethical (Moral) Behaviour:** The final stage in the four-step model of ethical decision-making is to engage in some behaviour in regard to the ethical dilemma. Research shows that behavioural intentions are the strongest predictor of actual behaviour in general, and ethical behaviour in particular.

However, individuals do always behave consistent with either their judgements or intentions in regard to ethical issues. This is particularly a problem in the business context, as peer group members, supervisors, and organisational culture may influence individuals to act in ways that are inconsistent with their own moral judgements and behavioural intentions.

## 2.6.3 Factors Affecting Ethical Decision-making

In general, there are three types of influences on ethical decision-making in business:

**1. Individual Difference Factors:** Individual difference factors are personal factors about an individual that may influence their sensitivity to ethical issues, their judgement about such issues, and their related behaviour. Research has identified many personal characteristics that impact ethical decision-making. The individual difference factor that has received the most research support is 'cognitive moral development.'

This framework, developed by Lawrence Kohlberg in the 1960s and extended by Kohlberg and other researchers in the subsequent years, helps to explain why different people make different evaluations when confronted with the same ethical issue. It posits that an individual's level of 'moral development' affects their ethical issue recognition, judgement, behavioural intentions, and behaviour.

According to this theory, the individuals' level of moral development passes through stages as they mature. Theoretically, there are three major levels of development. The lowest level of moral development is termed the 'pre-conventional' level. At the two stages of this level, the individual typically will evaluate ethical issues in the light of a desire to avoid punishment and/or seek personal reward. The pre-conventional level of moral development is usually associated with small children or adolescents.

The middle level of development is called the 'conventional' level. At the stages of the conventional level, the individual assesses ethical issues on the basis of the fairness to others and a desire to conform to societal rules and expectations. Thus, the individual concerned looks outside him or her to determine what is right and wrong. According to Kohlberg, most adults operate at the conventional level of moral reasoning.

The highest stage of moral development is the 'principled' level. In this level, the individual is likely to apply principles (which may be utilitarian, deontological, or justice) to ethical issues in an attempt to resolve them. According to Kohlberg, a principled person looks inside him or herself and is less likely to be influenced by situational (organisational) expectations.

The cognitive moral development framework is relevant to business ethics because it offers a powerful explanation of individual differences in ethical reasoning. The individuals at different levels of moral development are likely to think differently about ethical issues and resolve them differently.

**2. Situational (Organisational) Factors:** The individuals' ethical issue recognition, judgement, and behaviour are affected by contextual factors. In the business ethics context, the organisational factors that affect ethical decision-making includes, the work group, the supervisor, organisational policies and procedures, organisational codes of conduct, and the overall organisational culture. Each of these factors, individually and collectively, can cause individuals to reach different conclusions about ethical issues than they would have on their own. This section looks at one of these organisational factors, codes of conduct, in more detail.

The codes of conduct are formal policies, procedures, and enforcement mechanisms that spell out the moral and ethical expectations of the given organisation. A key part of organisational codes of conduct are written ethics codes. In other words, ethics codes are statements of the norms and beliefs of an organisation. These norms and beliefs are generally proposed, discussed, and defined by the senior executives of the firm concerned. Whatever process is used for their determination, the norms and beliefs are then disseminated throughout the firm.

Almost all large companies and many small companies have ethics codes. However, in and of themselves, ethics codes are unlikely to influence individuals to be more ethical in the conduct of business. To be effective, ethics codes must be part of a value system that permeates the culture of the organisation. The executives must display genuine commitment to the ideals expressed in the written code – if their behaviour is inconsistent with the formal code, the code's effectiveness will be reduced considerably.

At the least, the code of conduct must be specific to the ethical issues confronted in the particular industry or company. It should be the subject of ethics training that focuses on actual dilemmas likely to be faced by employees in an organisation. The conduct code must contain communication mechanisms for the dissemination of the organisational ethical standards and for the reporting of perceived wrongdoing within the organisation by the employees concerned.

The organisations must also ensure that perceived ethical violations are adequately investigated and that wrongdoing is punished. Research suggests that unless ethical behaviour is rewarded and unethical behaviour punished, the written codes of conduct are unlikely to be of much use.

**3. Issue-Related Factors:** The conceptual research by Thomas Jones in the 1990s and subsequent empirical studies suggest that ethical issues in business must have a certain level of 'moral intensity' before they will trigger ethical decision-making processes. Thus, individual and situational factors are unlikely to influence decision-making for issues considered by the individual to be minor.

Certain characteristics of issues determine their moral intensity. In general, the research suggests that issues with more serious consequences are more likely to reach the threshold level of intensity. Likewise, issues that are deemed by a societal consensus to be ethical or unethical are more likely to trigger ethical decision-making processes.

In summary, business ethics is an exceedingly complicated area, one that has contemporary significance for all business practitioners. There are, however, guidelines in place for effective ethical decision-making. These all have their positive and negative sides to them, but taken together, they may assist the business person to steer toward the most ethical decision possible under a particular set of circumstances.

## 2.7 Professional Ethics

Professions are vocations which specially involve some branch of advanced learning or science, such as medicine, law and engineering. The members of such professions are highly acclaimed for their special knowledge, skill and experience. Social prestige and wealth are their rewards. The modern world and particularly corporate business world, accords them many special privileges considering their contribution to society. They are allowed to identify themselves as professions; they are allowed to be self-governing or largely autonomous with special ethical responsibilities. They have evolved professional ethical codes which they are privileged to impose on themselves.

The role of the professions in business bears scrutiny. The activities of professional organisations also need to be examined. As some of them are self-employed, it will be necessary to examine the professions as independent businesses.

Professional ethics helps a professional choose what to do when faced with a problem at work that raises a moral issue.

### 2.7.1 Professions and Professionalism

The use of the words 'profession' and 'professional' is rather confusing. A professional, as opposed to an amateur, (as in 'an amateur boxer or cricketer') is a person who is engaged in a specified activity as one's main paid occupation. It also means a person who earns his living by practising some skill or engaging in some activity that requires some expertise, but which others do as a hobby in their spare time. Such are professional carpenters, plumbers, bricklayers, painters, cooks, and so on. There are professional actors and actresses, writers, painters, athletes, and so on, who take a certain pride in their chosen vocation, and work full time, for payment. But not all these activities qualify as 'professions', in the particular sense in which a surgeon, a physician, or even a chartered accountant is spoken of. They are tradesmen practising some useful craft accessible to all, modestly paid, and with modest recognition.

A 'professional' or a member of modern 'professions' is compared to 'a witch doctor' of ancient times. He has some special arcane or 'mysterious' knowledge (accessible to only a few) which he uses for the benefit of society. In return for it, he commands great respect and prestige, and the privilege of initiating his successor into his role. These characteristics are seen in the modern professions of medicine, law, engineering, architecture, and even accounting, and so on. In the old days, priests, soldiers (officers) were regarded as professions along with the medical profession.

The modern professionals (like, the members of the medical and legal professions) receive deservedly high prestige, respect, social status, and autonomy, besides considerable wealth. Hence, it is not surprising that more and more groups aspire to gain recognition as professions to enjoy the privileges of rank.

Those apart, the professions enjoy a great degree of autonomy, and therein lies their secret of high status in society. They set their own standards, decide upon the course content of their subjects of study, regulate entry into their profession, determine the period of time of learning and training necessary, discipline their own members, and generally function with fewer restrictions than others.

They set their own task, undergo no supervision, and do not need to punch time clocks. In return for such large autonomy, society expects them to serve the public good, to set a higher standard of conduct for themselves as compared to what is required of other men. Also, they are expected to enforce higher discipline on themselves and their fellow members. Less social control necessarily entails greater self-control and self-regulation. Those groups which wish to gain the status and privileges of a profession organise themselves into a professional association and promulgate a code of professional ethical conduct. It will be necessary to examine how it appears on a closer scrutiny.

### 2.7.2 Professional Ethical Codes

There are two arguments in favour of giving autonomy to a profession. First, the special nature of knowledge that they have mastered: it is highly specialised, and obtained after a hard and dedicated study and training after many years, and not easily mastered by the laymen, and is of the highest benefit for society. The second argument is that the members of the profession themselves set higher standards for themselves than what society would require of its laymen citizens, businessmen and others.

The profession is in every way knowledgeable about its members' activities, and can be alert to violations of the standards set, and thereby, the body will be in a proper position to censure and dismiss from its ranks those who do not live up to the profession's code of ethics.

Society responds positively to such demands. It needs the services of doctors, who are competent, trustworthy, and concerned enough to go beyond the duty's call to help the patients. All that the society would insist upon is that only the competent should be allowed to practice medicine: and hence, the need for proof of training, knowledge, competence, and character, and thus, it gives them a proper licence to practice. The state issues the licence but the body to decide upon the competence and skill is the professional association. This gives rise to a conflict of interests, because of confused role assignment.

Since the knowledge is technical, the candidate is examined by doctors or doctor representatives; the curriculum is set by them; they control the entry of students depending upon the capacity of the medical schools to handle them; they will decide who are to be admitted to which course; what they will learn and who will be allowed to practice; they set the standards of practice. Thus, the entire medical course and the nation's healthcare industry are controlled, guided and decided by the professional medical associations. Similarly, lawyers control legal education, bar examinations and the standards of the legal education. The same goes for the Chartered Accountants.

As these groups control entry into the field, set the standards and make policies for operating in the field, these groups act as monopolies, and exercise monopolistic power.

The reason why a given society allows these groups special privileges and monopolistic power is not difficult to work out. The professions set themselves higher standards than society ever sets for others. In the past, this practically meant that their norms went beyond the call of ordinary duty.

For instance, doctors were expected to serve patients who could not pay. Lawyers would be willing to serve clients who could not pay for their services, only in the interest of justice and helping the poor. Such behaviour was not expected of a businessman or a shopkeeper or tradesman. Secondly, doctors would be at the beck and call of any person who needed their service, being stricken ill suddenly, or meeting with an accident. They were expected to work as long as necessary without any time limit. Their knowledge and skill were an evergreen offering laid at the service of society. Thirdly, the members were expected to follow a higher standard of ethics in both their personal as well as professional level. They were expected to set an example for others in society, by keeping themselves above board in all their dealings. In other words, they are expected to be role models for the others in society.

Their special knowledge and skill, dedication to work, and exemplary conduct in personal and professional life, confers on them prestige, power, respect, and autonomy in their societal dealings.

There is much justification to say that the benefits and privileges a profession seeks become legitimate to the extent that the members live up to a higher moral code than do ordinary citizens.

When we speak of moral obligations of a given profession, we imply that every member of such profession has the obligation to live upto the standards set by the body and, in addition, to see to it that all the other members do so. The moral status of the professions can be rightly compared with those of corporations and corporate responsibility. Being a member of a constituted, self-regulated, properly defined group entails the individual member to accept and honour the moral obligations of the group in his individual as well as community role.

In simple words, the profession has the moral obligation to make sure that medical care is available to all, without exception. The same goes for the other well-constituted professional bodies. Their services must be made available to all members of society. This is where the role of professional ethical codes fits in precisely.

It is a fact that professions no longer set higher moral standards for themselves. What they set are professional standards called sometimes 'ethical standards'. These have little to do with moral standards. In other words, the professional standards do not necessarily translate into moral standards. Their claims are manifold: that they know the proper role members of their profession should play in society; that they set high professional standards to protect society from quacks, frauds, and incompetent persons; that they know the devious and sharp practices to which members of their professions resort to at times; that they know the means by which immoral and unethical practices are made without the knowledge of the public. The special knowledge which is exclusively possessed by the members may lead some of them into temptation at the cost of the general public. Such persons can be restrained best by the insiders who have comparable knowledge. It is as the saying goes: **'It takes a diamond to cut diamond'**. The argument, therefore, goes like this - the professions should be given autonomy and allowed to be self-regulating, because they are best equipped to know how their colleagues and peers act, and are in a good position to judge whether they act properly or improperly.

If their arguments are accepted, then, a society would have to allow all other similar professions to act with autonomy and self-regulation. But the crux of the matter is the ethical nature of their claim, as stated in their professional ethical codes.

The question is whether the common man would be able to understand if he is getting good service from his doctor or not. The layman, while not claiming specialist knowledge like, a doctor, is still able to sense when his doctor is unsure of himself; when his doctor is not forthcoming with all the facts; when a wrong diagnosis has been possibly made; or, when the treatment is inappropriate. The ordinary people can judge certain aspects of medical practice and their results as applicable to them. The doctor's expertise is not as exclusive as claimed. The same goes for the lawyers. In fact, in the USA, the ordinary citizens sit in judgement as members of jury. They master the technical facts of the case, or can get the case explained in a non-technical manner. Still, they can make an intelligent judgement on the issue. All these point out to the fact that although the members of a profession know their profession inside out, it still does not grant them the exclusive right to autonomy.

Self-regulation becomes justifiable only if a society is satisfied that the profession is policing itself effectively, and its code requires higher moral standards than non-professional occupations. In other words, self-regulation is justified only when the members of a society live up to their code of ethics in all their sincerity to promote the general good. Only under these conditions, the professions may be granted full autonomy, and their professional ethical codes could claim to be ethical.

There is an inherent conflict of interests in the restrictions placed on entry into the medical profession. No doubt, the restrictions become necessary depending upon the facilities for training new doctors. But, on the flip side, the restrictions that are in place also may in a way enable the existing doctors to claim higher fees for their services. In other words, for their own vested interests, they might support such restrictions. For many years, there has been a shortage of doctors in many parts of the country, especially, where the poor people are concentrated as in rural areas and city slums. Moreover, in the advanced countries, doctors trained in the Third World find it difficult to be licensed. Due to this, there is an acute dearth of quality medical care and services across the world. This situation is all the more baffling since there is available a large pool of competent applicants for medical education. Therefore, a question arises as to whether or not the profession is collectively discharging its responsibility – that of providing doctors for all sectors of society. Even on an individual level, the members of the medical profession cannot ignore their moral obligation to serve all sectors of society. This applies more so in the case of disadvantaged sections, which have been for various reasons, remained out of the ambit of preventive medical help and education. In the light of the aforesaid scenario, it would be highly improper, in the ethical sense, for a service profession like, medicine, to charge or receive higher fees for their services. In the good old days, a doctor was equated to God in India: *Vaidyo Narayano Hari.*

### 2.7.3 Analysis of a Professional Ethical Codes

The present day professional codes of conduct serve many different purposes other than stating a higher moral standard. It serves a ceremonial purpose, as for instance, when it is read out and repeated solemnly by new members upon initiation. Some codes set a set of ideals to which the members must aspire and by which they should be guided. Failure to attain the goals is expected, and few ever actually achieve the goal stated. The third variety of codes is disciplinary.

They state the minimum of the conditions that the members are to subscribe to. Failure to maintain the minimum standard will call for sanctions, the most severe of which is expulsion. The fourth type of codes states the professional etiquette. In fact, a single code may include a statement of ideals, a set of disciplinary rules, and standards of professional etiquette.

### 2.7.4 Characteristics of a Professional Ethical Code

A profession which claims autonomy from the non-professional social control must not only display an exemplary moral standard but also encode the same in its Professional Ethical Code. The minimum requirements would, therefore, be the following:

1. The code should specify clearly which parts are ideals, and which are to be considered as regulative norms. The norms should be clearly and unambiguously available to the public, and they should be higher than other norms of society.

2. The code should protect the interests of those served by the profession, as well as the interests of the public.

3. The code should be specific and honest: this means that it should deal specifically with those problems of the profession that pose temptation to its members. Unless the code seeks to deal with the gray areas, like, the potential unethical and often illegal practices in an honest manner, it will not be able to prove the commitment of the members of the profession for public welfare and common good.

4. The code should avoid self-serving efforts. Setting fees and restricting advertisements are matters which may be of interest for the members in an egoistic sense, but may not be so for the general public. For example, the code provisions preventing competition are not in the larger public interest. It is so, since they emphasise the negative, monopolistic nature of the professions and, therefore, are better avoided.

5. The code must be not only be policeable but also should be positively policed. The code must have provisions for bringing charges and applying penalties. Otherwise, it will end up as a diluted version of some high-sounding ideals.

A profession seeking autonomy, public respect and special privileges must demonstrate by its record that it has a vital and effective self-regulatory mechanism in place, and, that it polices its own rank effectively without fear or favour for upholding the higher than normal moral principles both in practice and precept. Otherwise, a society will find little justification to allow it special privileges. On the other hand, a society will appropriately make legislation to control the activities of that profession as it usually does in the case of other occupations.

Although professions can enforce their codes on their members, it must be noted that they are not courts of law. Therefore, violations of codes can only be subjected to limited discipline, the severest penalty being expulsion, accompanied by public exposure. Censure, however, remains the most frequent penalty.

The professional codes are applicable to all member-professionals regardless of whether they work for themselves or for an employer. The codes may set a higher standard than the employer (company) allows. This is another gray area of ethical conduct.

## 2.8 Gandhian Philosophy of Ethical Behaviour

Mahatma Gandhi's life and works and speeches are saturated with his ethical idiosyncrasies. Every single issue that he has examined and got involved with exudes morality and ethics. This is found to be true in his analysis of the social system, exploitation and inequalities, conflict and conflict resolution, state, power and policy, development and underdevelopment and his economic analysis. In what follows, we will concentrate on a few important ethical issues which are critical in the understanding of Gandhian philosophy.

**Truth, Non-violence and Religion: The Basic Axioms :**

It needs to be mentioned in the analysis of the Gandhian ethics that, according to Gandhi, truth and non-violence are interrelated categories. Gandhian ethics is mainly based no four nomological axioms. These are truth, non-violence, *anasakti* (non-attachment to worldly weather) and *sarvodaya* (welfare of all). Gandhi considered some crucial institutional parameters which included families, communities and tradiational socio-religious institutions like *varnashram* (social division of labour) as ordained by religious tradition. The social division of labour suggests social interdependence through the traditional *jajmani system*. He wanted to introduce many institutional changes to achieve the goal of an ideal society. These institutional changes include the introduction of bread-labour, trusteeship, spiritualisation of politics and so forth.

**Bread labour** was a term popularised by Gandhi, such labour needs to be done by everybody irrespective of one's or status in life. It gives an opportunity to participate in the fulfillment of the universal law of *karma* (action) and recognise the significance of the dignity of labour.

**Trusteeship** is a system of reforming the capitalist organisations. The Gandhian system of trusteeship is based on the idea that the rich people and the capitalists should considered that, a part of their wealth should be distributed to the society for the maximisation of social welfare. Trusteeship is an attempt to socialise wealth and to allow social control over poverty and economic inequalities in a country like India where the distribution of income and wealth is highly skewed. The principle of trusteeship is to reinforce the spirit of the philosophy of renunciation and sacrifice.

The two most important **categorical imperatives** in the Gandhian ethics are non-violence and truth. *Satyagraha* (adherence to truth), like non-violence, remains **both a mean and an end** in itself. Gandhi observed that individual welfare and social welfare are interdependent in nature and the former is contained in the latter. To Gandhi, the basic desideratum of all social action and policy is the maximisation of social welfare. The welfare is not predicated upon the material sense of the term but is more of a spiritual nature. For him, wealth does not mean welfare. Gandhi thought that it is necessary to voluntarily reduce wants, particularly when a majority of the people are not really living but somehow exist below the poverty line. All economic activities should, according to Gandhi, be based on ethical and moral considerations. Gandhi' economics is pragmatic yet moral.

## Exploitation, Inequalities and Injustice:

Gandhi observed that it is possible to remove all types of exploitation through the development of a strong will power. Exploitation and inequalities are interrelated in the Gandhian ethics. Gandhi believes that "our ignorance or negligence of the Divine Law, which gives to man from day to day his daily bread and n more, has given rise to inequalities with all the miseries attendant upon them" **(Gandhi, 1930, 26 August)**. To minimise the degree of inequalities in society, Gandhi advocated a twofold **affirmative action programme**; first, to reduce the range of inequalities through various actions and policies; to eliminate the chance of the growth of inequalities in future. Gandhi was sufficiently pragmatic to realise that in a modern society with a predominantly materialistic culture, economic inequality will stay on. It is also true that some inequalities are natural. For the remove of some economic inequalities under capitalism, a non-violent action is preferable to the violent enforcement of egalitarian principles because such actions will only kill the goose that lays the golden egg. Gandhi also favoured a **distributive justice** for educing inequalities and exploitation.

## Conflict and Conflict Resolution:

Gandhi's theory of conflict resolution is an attempt to ensure justice in the deal and to establish the region of justice. The retreat to justice is both the means and the end in his theory of conflict management. Through the operation of the principle of justice in the matter of conflict resolution, he wished to achieve at least three proximate objectives – to put an end to the conflict arising out of horizontal and vertical inequalities, to assign appropriate rights and freedom to the repressed weaker section of the community and to weed out the constraints in the way of human development and capability expansion of all classes of people. This was necessary for *sarvodaya* – the highest stage of Gandhian socialism. Gandhi suggested four basic methods for conflict resolution – negotiations and persuasion, *satyagraha*, education and organisational institutional reforms.

For conflict resolution, Gandhi suggested a mutual co-operation between the parties. If the co-operative conflict is the aim, as in the case of the Gandhian theory of conflict resolution, then both the workers and the capitalist will work hard to maximise the profit of the company. Gandhi put more emphasis on the benefits from co-operation. Negotiations may not always guarantee the maximum pay-off but can be an important alternative to a deadlock. He is sure that both the parties can be at a maximum benefit if they have co-operation between them rather than confrontation.

## Rights and Duties:

Gandhi's balanced view on rights, duties and equalities is a contemporary remainder to those proponents of human rights and egalitarianism who purpose these rights unconditionally without any corresponding human duties. However, in the absence of human duties, human rights do not remain in a workable proposition in the long run. One such duty is the duty of constant pre-occupation with one's own work (deontic duty). In this context, Gandhi supported the **Kantian theory of deontology**. Gandhi was profoundly influenced by John Ruskin's book *Unto this Last* (1862), which considered all works to be of equal dignity. However, Gandhi advised that if any order or work suggested by the superior officer is unethical or immoral, one should not carry such a duty.

**Gandhi on Sustainable Development:**

Gandhi realised that although economic development was necessary for a country like India, capitalist industrialisation was unwanted industrialisation leads to either active or passive exploitation of villagers. Capital-intensive methods of industrialisation also lead to the impoverishment of villages and an increase in unemployment. Moreover, capitalist development breeds a permanent conflict between labour and capital. It is because of the possibility of inequality that Gandhi did not want industrialisation. Through economic development, Gandhi wanted to generate rejuvenation of mind, body and spirit for everybody.

Gandhi was not in favour of an exorbitantly high rate of growth of output *per se*, but he wanted a fairly good amount of production to satisfy the increased rate of population growth. He was right in appreciating the truth that a high rate of growth is not necessarily the optimum rate of growth. Gandhi advocated the control of desire for meta-needs and bringing down the scale of wants to the *ethical minima* or what can be called the *basic necessities of life*. This is necessary in the content of the staggering poverty of India and it requires some changes in lifestyle. These basic necessities include people's right to a proper house, an adequate and balanced diet for the family and the supply of locally made clothes, facilities for the education of children and adequate medical relief. To Gandhi, economic development does not mean that one should have more but that one should be more. His concept of development is ethical in nature in the sense that it incorporates social well-being, human capability expansion, equality of opportunity, justice and non-exploitation and rights and freedom (See Fig. 2.1).

The production of basic needs has to be employment-generating and income-creating and what was needed was mutual help and cooperation without exploitation at the levels of both production and distribution. In the Gandhian schema, sustainable development must have a moral basis. It needs discipline and moral responsibility as well as a particular type of personality pattern. The production conditions of the basic necessities of life would be under the direct control of the people. Rural development was through to be means for correcting the urban bias. Gandhi's main argument for the development of village industries was to remove poverty through the generation of sufficient employment opportunities for the unemployed, underemployed and surplus (idle) labour.

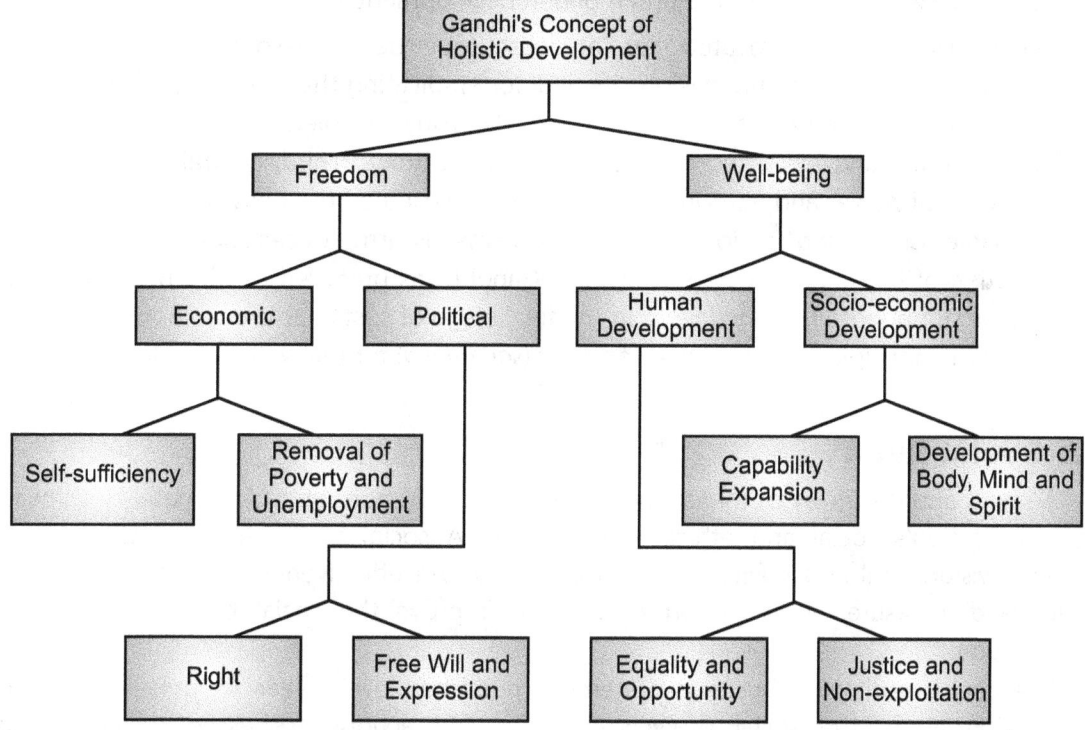

**Fig. 2.1: Gandhi's Concept of Holistic Development**

The Gandhian type of sustainable development seems to be feasible and realistic, given the basic objective functions, the possible parameters of action and the economic milieu of his time.

In Gandhi's view, technological improvement could be introduced to the village industries to make capital more efficient. In fact, an appropriate technology was needed for the regeneration of village economy and such technology would not be an anachronism but could be well embedded in the system. In the case of "Gandhian development", the basic objective being full employment even with a low level of per capita income and economic independence with social justice, the appropriate technique of production could not have been anything other than the labour-intensive method.

The more advanced stage of development in Gandhian plan would be marked by an increasing degree of decentralisation of the industrial structure which was initiated in the first stage of rural development. Gandhi advocated decentralisation for reaping the advantages resulting out of the flexible structure of technology and organisation. Decentralisation was not meant for capital goods but only for consumer goods industries. Decentralisation was not only recommended for industries but also for political power in order to make it more advantageous for the common people. The decentralised structure of the politico-economic system was presumed to be necessary for preventing exploitation, inequality and conflicts. The structure change suggested in the second stage of development after the attainment of self-sufficiency was to eradicate the urban bias in development.

Decentralisation is advocated for at least four basic reasons. First, for better administration, control and supervision. Second, for eradicating the possibility of violence, as centralised organisation or institutions are generally prone to violence. Centralisation cannot be fully defended and protected without an adequate force. Third, centralisation leads to concentration of power and authority which can be misused by the possessor of such power in the name of settling socio-economic problems. Fourth, decentralisation stands for maximisation of individual freedom. However, Gandhi was prepared to give more power to people's organisations like *panchayats*. In the final stage of sustainable development, Gandhi suggested the principle of holistic development (*sarvodaya*) for the welfare of all.

## 2.9 Social Audit

A social audit is a way of measuring, understanding, reporting and ultimately improving an organisation's social and ethical performance. A social audit helps to narrow gaps between vision/goal and reality, between efficiency and effectiveness. It is a technique to understand, measure, verify, report on and to improve the social performance of the organisation.

The social audit is a business statement published every year to present a set of information about the social projects, benefits and actions addressed to employees, investors, market analysts, shareholders and the community at large. It also functions as a strategic instrument to evaluate the practice of corporate social responsibility.

Through its social audit the company shows what it does on behalf of its professional staff, their families, collaborators and the community at large. Transparency is given to the activities developed to improve quality of life. Its main function is to make public the company's social responsibility, thereby strengthening the links between company, society and environment.

When put together by multiple professionals, the social audit shows and measures the company's concern about people and about life in our planet.

Social audit is thus a formal review of a company's endeavours in social responsibility. A social audit looks at factors such as a company's record of charitable giving, volunteer activity, energy use, transparency, work environment and worker pay and benefits to evaluate what kind of social and environmental impact a company is having in the locations where it operates. Social audits are optional - companies can choose whether to perform them and whether to release the results publicly or only use them internally.

Social auditing creates an impact upon governance. It values the voice of stakeholders, including marginalised/poor groups whose voices are rarely heard. Social auditing is taken up for the purpose of enhancing local governance, particularly for strengthening accountability and transparency in local bodies.

The key difference between development and social audit is that a social audit focuses on the neglected issue of social impacts, while a development audit has a broader focus including environment and economic issues, such as the efficiency of a project or programme.

**Objectives of Social Audit**

In the era of corporate social responsibility, where corporations are often expected not just to deliver value to consumers and shareholders but also to meet environmental and social standards deemed desirable by some vocal members of the general public, social audits can help companies create, improve and maintain a positive public relations image. Good public relations are key because the way a company is perceived will usually have an impact on its bottom line.

1. Assessing the physical and financial gaps between needs and resources available for local development.
2. Creating awareness among beneficiaries and providers of local, social and productive services.
3. Increasing efficacy and effectiveness of local development programmes.
4. Scrutiny of various policy decisions, keeping in view stakeholder interests and priorities, particularly of rural poor.
5. Estimation of the opportunity cost for stakeholders of not getting timely access to public services.

**Features of Social Audit**

The features of Social Audit are discussed below:
1. The areas for social audit include any activity which has a significant social impact, such as activities affecting environmental quality, consumerism, opportunities for women and other disadvantaged people in society and similar others.
2. Normally, the social audit is that it can determine only what an organisation is doing in social areas, not the amount of social good that results from these activities. It is a process audit rather than audit for results.
3. Auditing social performance is very difficult because most of the results of social activities occur beyond the companies limit.
4. Both quantitative and qualitative data are essential for social audit to evaluate the organisations social performance.

**The Scope of Social Audit**

A social audit will generally examine the organisation's policies and practices in the following key areas:
1. **Ethics:** What the organisation's policies are, whether or not they are being upheld or undermined by the enterprise's day-to-day activities.
2. **Staffing:** How the enterprise rewards, trains and develops its staff, as well as the way in which the enterprise ensures that it is non-discriminatory, fair and equitable to everyone working there.

3. **Environment:** The enterprise's policies relating to caring for the environment, waste management and disposal, and damage reduction, and whether or not the enterprise is adhering to these policies.
4. **Human Rights:** How it ensures that it does not violate human rights, or deal, trade with or support any organisation that violates human rights.
5. **Community:** The organisation's policies relating to the local community, and community involvement; these policies might, for example, cover community partnerships or community projects, and checks will be made during the social audit to ensure that agreements are being upheld.
6. **Society:** The organisation's policies relating to society as a whole, and the way in which the enterprise seeks to improve or benefit society.
7. **Compliance:** How the organisation complies with statutory and legal requirements, such as health and safety, employment law, environmental law, criminal law and, of course, financial and tax laws.

### Advantages of Social Audit

1. Trains the community on participatory local planning.
2. Encourages local democracy.
3. Encourages community participation.
4. Benefits disadvantaged groups.
5. Promotes collective decision making and sharing responsibilities.
6. Develops human resources and social capital

### Essentials of Social Audit

To be effective, the social auditor must have the right to:
1. Seek clarifications from the implementing agency about any decision-making, activity, scheme, income and expenditure incurred by the agency;
2. Consider and scrutinise existing schemes and local activities of the agency; and
3. Access registers and documents relating to all development activities undertaken by the implementing agency or by any other government department.

This requires transparency in the decision-making and activities of the implementing agencies. In a way, social audit includes measures for enhancing transparency by enforcing the right to information in the planning and implementation of local development activities.

## Points to Remember

1. "**Corporate or organisational ethics**" refers to the generally accepted standards that guide behaviour in business and other organisational contexts.

2. **Ten Commandments of ethical business behaviour are:**
   - Be honest, truthful, forthright, candid and sincere.
   - Have integrity: Strive to be scrupulous.
   - Keep your word and abide by the spirit as well as the letter of the law.
   - Maintain fidelity: Be faithful and never disclose confidential information.
   - Always be fair: Demonstrate a commitment to justice, with equal treatment of all.
   - Care for others: Be kind.
   - Respect others in every way.
   - Be a responsible citizen. Obey just laws and protest unjust ones.
   - Rigorously pursue excellence. Never be content with mediocrity.
   - Always be accountable: Good leaders lead by example.
3. **Individual ethics** are the generally accepted principles of right and wrong governing the conduct of individuals.
4. **Professional ethics** helps a professional choose what to do when faced with a problem at work that raises a moral issue.
5. **Corporate ethics** apply to all aspects of business conduct, including board strategies, how companies treat employees and suppliers, sales and marketing techniques and accounting practices.

## Questions for Discussion

1. What are individual or personal ethics? Explain the importance of individual ethics in relation with business ethics.
2. What are the salient features of professional ethical codes? Give an example from the medical field.
3. Should "professionals" be obliged to fall in line with the code of conduct of society in general?
4. State the types of business ethics. Discuss the factors influencing business ethics.
5. What is meant by corporate codes? What are its limitations?
6. What are the virtues of corporate codes?
7. Write a note on corporate code formal committees.
8. Is ethical audit feasible? If so, how? Give examples.
9. Give a formal model of an ethical audit.
10. Write a note on :
    (a) Professional ethical code.
    (b) Professions and professionalism.
    (c) Social audit.
    (d) Characteristics of a professional ethical code.

# Chapter 3...
# Business Ethics in a Global Economy

## Contents ...

- 3.1 Introduction
- 3.2 Concept of Globalisation
- 3.3 Global Business Network
  - 3.3.1 Cultural Issues
  - 3.3.2 Legal Issues
  - 3.3.3 Accountability Issues
- 3.4 Relationship among Business, Business Ethics and Business Development
  - 3.4.1 Unfair or Deceptive Business Development Practices
  - 3.4.2 Offensive Materials and Objectionable Business Development Practices
  - 3.4.3 Ethical Product and Distribution Practices
  - 3.4.4 Does Business Development Overfocus on Materialism?
  - 3.4.5 Special Ethical Issues in Marketing to Children
  - 3.4.6 Ethical Issues in Business Development to Minorities
  - 3.4.7 Ethical Issues Surrounding the Portrayal of Women in Business Development Efforts
- 3.5 Developing Business Ethics in a Global Economy
  - 3.5.1 Global Ethical Issues
  - 3.5.2 Global Institutes Providing Help in Ethical Implementation
  - 3.5.3 Guidelines to Ensure Code of Ethics for Global Business
- 3.6 Marketing Ethics in Foreign Trade
- 3.7 Role of Business Ethics in Developing a Civilised Society
  - 3.7.1 Environmental Perspectives
  - 3.7.2 Economic Perspectives
  - 3.7.3 Social Perspectives
  - • Points to Remember
  - • Questions for Discussion

## Learning Objectives ...

> ➤ To be aware of the concept of globalisation
> ➤ To be able to discuss the impact of Global Business Network
> ➤ To examine the relationship among Business, Business Ethics and Business Development
> ➤ To explore the development of business ethics in a global economy
> ➤ To look at the role of business ethics in developing a civilised society

## 3.1 Introduction

Globalisation has become one of the most prominent buzzwords of recent times. In the business community, in particular, there has been considerable enthusiasm about globalisation.

At the same time, however, business leaders have also started to recognise the increased risks that globalisation can bring to their operations. This shows that globalisation clearly has some downsides, even for the business community.

In the context of business ethics, this controversy over globalisation plays a crucial role. After all, all corporations – most notably, the Multi National Corporations (MNCs) are at the centre of the public's criticism on globalisation. They are accused of exploiting the workers in developing countries, destroying the environment, abusing their economic power by engaging developing countries in a so-called 'race to the bottom'.

The term mentioned above describes a process whereby MNCs pitch developing countries against each other by allocating Foreign Direct Investment (FDI) to those countries that can offer them the most favourable conditions in terms of low tax rates, low levels of environmental regulation, and restricted workers' rights. However true these accusations are in practice, there is no doubt that globalisation is the most demanding of arenas of today's times in which corporations have to define and legitimise the 'right or wrong' of their behaviour.

## 3.2 Concept of Globalisation

Globalisation is not only a very controversial topic, it is also often a fiercely contested term in academic discourse. Globalisation is a process that has been going on for the past 5,000 years, but it has significantly accelerated since the dismantling of the Soviet Union as a Republic in 1991.

In considering the history of globalisation, some authors focus on events since the discovery of the America in 1492, but most scholars and theorists prefer to concentrate on the more recent past. But long before 1492, people began to link together disparate locations in the world into extensive systems of communication, migration, and interconnections. This formation of interaction between the global and the local has been a central driving force in the world history.

Economic globalisation means that world trade and financial markets are becoming more integrated. According to Friedman (1999), Globalisation is:

*"The inexorable integration of markets, nation states, and technologies to a degree never witnessed before - in a way that is enabling individuals, corporations and nation-states to reach around the world farther, faster, deeper and cheaper than before, the spread of free-market capitalism to virtually every country in the world".*

On the other hand, a great number of economists assert that globalisation, as an ongoing historical process that reached its apex toward the end of the 20$^{th}$ century. This process leads to the increasing integration of the production of goods, services, ideas, culture, communication and environmental pollution on a world-wide scale, imparting locality of populations and labour.

Some argue that there is nothing like a 'global' economy, because roughly ninety per cent of the world trade only takes place either within or between the three economic blocks of the EU, North America, and East Asia, leaving out all other major parts of the globe (Chortarea and Pelagidis 2004; World Trade Organisation 2004). Obviously, we have to examine the buzzword 'globalisation' more carefully and to develop a more precise definition if we want to understand its character and its implication for business ethics.

From the economical point of view, two macro factors seem to underlie the trend toward globalisation (Frankel, 2000). The first is the decline in barriers to flow of goods, services and capital that has occurred since the end of World War II. The second factor is technological change, particularly, the dramatic developments in recent years in communication, information processing, and transportation technologies.

Everybody knows the importance of the role technological innovations and developments in globalisation. On the other hand, 'declining trade and investment barriers' with the help of GATT and WTO is as important as the first one.

Scholte (2000 : 46–61) characterises globalisation as 'deterritorialisation', suggesting that we can define globalisation as follows:

*"Globalisation is the progressive eroding of the relevance of territorial bases for social, economic and political activities, processes and relations."*

In consonance with the aforesaid definition, the following examples can be cited :

- Due to the availability of modern communication infrastructure, many of us could actually witness the 2006 Fifa World Cup in Germany live on TV – regardless of where we were located at that time. This event was global not in the sense that it actually happened all over the world, but in the sense, that billions of people saw it, and to some extent took part in it, regardless of the fact that they were standing in Milan, Manchester, or Manila.

- We can potentially drink the same Heineken beer, drive the same model of Toyota car, or buy the same expensive Rolex watch almost wherever we are in the world – we do not have to be in Amsterdam, Tokyo, or Geneva. Certain global products are available all over the world and going for a 'Chinese', 'Mexican', or 'French' meal indicates certain tastes and styles rather than a trip to a certain geographical territory.

- We no longer tend to worry about where our bank stores our money and if their 'safes' really deserve that name. We can quite easily have a credit card which allows us to withdraw money all over the world, we can pay our bills at home in Europe via internet banking while sitting in an internet café in India, or even order our Swiss private banking broker to buy an option on halved pegs at the Chicago exchange without even moving our feet from the sofa.

We can conclude that globalisation is an economic and political phenomenon profoundly affecting the choices and the consequences of such choices of even the most locally determined institutions and individuals. Globalisation is not an option we can choose but rather an imperative we cannot ignore. However, rather than being an imperative that directly imposes duties, it, on the contrary, challenges one to discover how moral duty and ethical responsibility are still possible under the influence of these new global forces.

Global communications, global products, and global financial systems and capital markets are only the most striking examples of deterritorialisation in the world economy. There are many other areas where globalisation in this sense is a significant social, economic, and political process. As we shall now see, globalisation also has significant implications for business ethics.

Thus, globalisation is an umbrella term which possesses various dimensions. It can be related to every fields of daily life in the following ways:

- Economics – related to globalisation in trade, money, corporations, banking, capital,
- Political – science, governance, wars, peace, IGOS, NGOS, and regimes,
- Sociology - communities, conflict, classes, nations, agreements,
- Psychology - individuals as subjects and objects of global action,
- Anthropology - cultures overlapping, adapting, clashing, merging,
- Communications - information as knowledge and tools- internet,
- Geography - Everything provided it can be anchored in space.

Each of these social sciences looks at a special aspect of the whole system of interdependent parts that constitutes our world system. Each discipline constructs a concept of globalisation that reflects its special point of view.

## 3.3 Global Business Network

**Theodore Levitt** has argued that, due to the advent of modern communications and transport technologies, consumer tastes and preferences are becoming global, which, in turn, is giving impetus to the creation of global markets for standardised consumer products as well as global business networks. However, this position is regarded as extreme by many commentators, who argue that substantial differences still exist between countries.

As local companies increasingly engage in cross-border trade and investment, the managers need to recognise that the task of managing an international business differs from that of managing a purely domestic business in many ways. First of all, the differences come from the simple fact that countries are different insofar as their cultures, socio-economic and political systems, legal systems and levels of economic development go. Despite widespread globalisation, there still exist many big and enduring differences between the countries.

That apart, the differences between countries require different marketing approaches. For example, marketing a product in Brazil may require a different approach than marketing the product in Australia or Malaysia. In the same way, managing U.S. Workers might require different skills than managing Japanese workers; maintaining close relations with a particular level of government may be very important in The Republic of China and totally irrelevant in Germany.

As a global firm, sometimes, it is impossible to advertise a standardised advertising message in different countries. Because of the existence of differences in cultural and legal environments, for instance, it is illegal to use any comparative advertising in Germany. Whereas in many other countries, advertising on television is strictly controlled in many countries, for e.g., in Kuwait, the government controlled TV network allows only thirty-two minutes of advertising per day, in the evening.

In order to compete successfully in the international environment, the firms concerned can use four basic entry strategies: an international strategy, a multi-domestic strategy, a global strategy, and a transnational strategy (Bartlett and Ghoshal, 1989).

The firms pursuing an international strategy transfer the skills and products derived from distinctive competencies to foreign markets, while undertaking some limited local customisation. On the other hand, those firms pursuing a multi-domestic strategy customise their product offering, marketing strategy, and business strategy to national conditions.

While the firms pursuing a global strategy focus on reaping the cost reductions that come from experience curve effects and location economies. Finally, those pursuing a transnational strategy would invariably have to simultaneously focus on reducing costs, transferring skills and products, and boosting local responsiveness. However, implementing this strategy at the ground level is very difficult because of the simultaneous pressures from two-pronged factors of - cost reductions and local responsiveness.

The following are the main issues to be looked at from the global business ethics perspective:

### 3.3.1 Cultural Issues

As business becomes less fixed territorially, as a logical corollary, many corporations increasingly engage in overseas markets, suddenly find themselves confronted with new and diverse, sometimes, and even contradicting ethical demands.

Moral values, which were taken for granted in the home market, may get questioned as soon as corporations enter foreign markets. For example, attitudes to racial and gender diversity in Europe may differ significantly to those in Middle Eastern countries. Similarly, the Chinese people might regard it as more unethical to sack employees in times of economic downturns than would be typical in Europe. Again, whilst Europeans tend to regard child labour as strictly unethical, some Asian countries might have a more moderate approach.

The reason why there is a potential for such problems is that whilst globalisation results in the deterritorialisation of some processes and activities, in many cases, there still exists a close connection between the local culture, including, moral values and, a certain geographical region.

For example, Europeans largely disapprove of capital punishment, whilst many Americans appear to regard it as morally acceptable. Similarly, women can freely sunbathe topless on most European beaches; while in some states of America they can get fined for doing so. In Pakistan, they would be expected to cover up much more. This is one of the contradictions of globalisation: on the one hand, globalisation makes regional difference less important since it brings regions together and encourages a more uniform 'global culture'. On the other, in eroding the divisions of geographical distances, globalisation reveals economic, political, and cultural differences and confronts people with them. This dialectical or contradictory effect has been a growing subject matter for research over the past decade

### 3.3.2 Legal Issues

A second aspect is closely linked to the relation of ethics and law. The more economic transactions lose their connection to a certain regional territory, the more they escape the control of the respective national governments. The power of a government has traditionally been confined to a certain territory, for example, the French laws are only binding on French territory, UK laws on UK territory, and so on.

As soon as a company leaves its home territory and moves part of its production chain to, for example, a third world country, the legal framework becomes very different. Consequently, the managers can no longer simply rely on the legal framework when deciding on the right or wrong of certain business practices.

It (the business ethics), largely begins where the law ends, then, deterritorialisation increases the demand for business ethics because deterritorialised economic activities are beyond the control of national (territorial) governments;

For example, global financial markets are beyond the control of any national government, and the constant struggle of governments against issues, such as, child pornography on the internet shows the enormous difficulties in enforcing national laws in deterritorialised geographics.

### 3.3.3 Accountability Issues

Taking a closer look at global activities, one can easily identify corporations as the dominant actors on the global stage : MNCs own the mass media which influences much of the information and entertainment we are exposed to, they supply global products, they pay peoples' salaries, and they pay (directly or indirectly) much of the taxes that keep governments running. Furthermore, one could argue that MNCs are economically as powerful as many governments.

For example, the turnover of General Motors is almost the same as the GDP of Denmark. However, the Danish government has to be accountable to the Danish people and must face elections on a regular basis, the managers of General Motors are formally accountable only to the relatively small group of people who own shares in their company. The communities in the US, Brazil, or Germany that depend directly on General Motors' investment decisions, however, have next to no influence on the company and, unlike a regional or national government, General Motors is, at least in principle, not accountable to these constituencies.

What this means is that the more economic activities get deterritorialised, the less governments can control them, and the less they are open to democratic control of the affected people. Consequently, the call for direct (democratic) accountability of MNCs has grown louder during the last years, evidenced for example, by the anti-globalisation protests that we witness today. To put it simply, globalisation leads to a growing demand for *corporate accountability*.

The table below shows the stakeholder-wise ethical impacts of globalisation.

**Table 3.1: Examples of the Ethical Impacts of Globalisation on Different Stakeholder Groups**

| Stakeholders | Ethical Impacts of Globalisation |
|---|---|
| Shareholders | Globalisation provides potential for greater profitability, but also greater risks. Lack of regulation of global capital markets, leading to additional financial and instability. |
| Employees | Corporations outsource production to developing countries in order to reduce costs in global marketplace - this provides jobs but also raises the potential for exploitation of employees through poor working conditions. |
| Consumers | Global products provides social benefits to consumers across the globe but may also meet protects about cultural imperialism and westernisation. Globalisation can bring cheaper prices to customers, but vulnerable consumers in developing countries may also face the possibility of exploitation by MNCs. |
| Suppliers and competition | Supplies in developing countries face regulation from MNCs through supply chain management. Small scale indigenous competitors exposed to powerful global players. |
| Civil society (pressure groups, NGOs, local communities) | Global business activities bring the company in direct interaction to local communities with possibility for erosion of traditional community life; globally active pressure groups emerge with aim to 'police' the corporation in countries where governments are weak and tolerant. |
| Government and regulation | Globalisation weakens governments and increases the corporate responsibility for jobs, welfare, maintenance of ethical standards, etc. Globalisation also confronts governments with corporations from different cultural expectations about issues such as bribery, corruption, taxation and philanthropy. |

## 3.4 Relationship among Business, Business Ethics and Business Development

A study in Business Horizons magazine from Indiana University, found that customers increasingly base their buying decisions on whether they believe a company is ethical or not.

Practising ethics in business development means deliberately applying standards of fairness, or moral rights and wrongs, to the marketing decision-making, behaviour, and practice in the organisation.

In a market economy, a business may be expected to act in what it believes to be its own best interests. The purpose of business development is to create competitive advantage *vis-à-vis* one's rivals. An organisation achieves an advantage when it does a better job than its competitors at satisfying the product and service requirements of its target markets. Those organisations that develop a competitive advantage are able to satisfy the needs of both customers and the organisation.

As our economic system has become more successful at providing for needs and wants, there has been greater focus on organisations' adhering to ethical values rather than simply providing products. This focus has come about for two reasons. Firstly, when an organisation behaves ethically, the customers develop more positive attitudes about the firm, its products, and its services.

When business development practices deviate from standards that society considers acceptable, the market process becomes less efficient—sometimes, it is even interrupted. Not employing ethical business development practices may lead to dissatisfied customers, bad publicity, a lack of trust, lost business, or, even at times, legal action. Thus, most organisations are very sensitive to the needs and opinions of their customers and look for ways to protect their long-term interests.

Secondly, ethical abuses frequently lead to pressure (social or government) for institutions to assume greater responsibility for their actions. Since abuses do occur, some people believe that questionable business practices abound. As a result, consumer interest groups, professional associations, and self-regulatory groups exert considerable influence on business development. Calls for social responsibility have also subjected business development practices to a wide range of federal and state regulations designed to either protect consumer rights or to stimulate trade.

That apart, the Federal and State government agencies are charged both with enforcing the laws and creating policies to limit unfair business development practices. Because regulation cannot be developed to cover every possible abuse, organisations and industry groups often develop codes of ethical conduct or rules for behaviour to serve as a guide in decision-making. The American Marketing Association, for example, has developed a code of ethics. Self-regulation not only helps a firm avoid extensive government intervention; it also allows it to better respond to changes in market conditions. An organisation's long-term success and profitability depends on this ability to respond.

The several areas of concern in business development ethics are as follows:

### 3.4.1 Unfair or Deceptive Business Development Practices

Business development practices are deceptive if customers believe they will get more value from a product or service than they actually receive. Deception, which can take the form of a misrepresentation, omission, or misleading practice, can occur when working with any element of the marketing mix.

Since consumers are exposed to great quantities of information about products and firms today, they often become skeptical of marketing claims and selling messages and act to protect themselves from being deceived. Thus, when a product or service does not provide expected value, customers will often seek a different source.

Deceptive pricing practices cause customers to believe that the price they pay for some unit of value in a product or service is lower than it really is. The deception might take the form of making false price comparisons, providing misleading suggested selling prices, omitting important conditions of the sale, or making very low price offers available only when other items are purchased as well.

The promotional practices are considered deceptive, when the seller intentionally misstates how a product is constructed or performs, fails to disclose information regarding pyramid sales (a sales technique in which a person is recruited into a plan and then expects to make money by recruiting other people), or employs bait-and-switch selling techniques (a technique in which a business offers to sell a product or service, often at a lower price, in order to attract customers who are then encouraged to purchase a more expensive item).

False or greatly exaggerated product or service claims also fall under this category. When packages are intentionally mislabeled as to contents, size, weight, or use information, that constitutes deceptive packaging; selling hazardous or defective products without disclosing the dangers; failing to perform promised services, and not honouring warranty obligations – *et al* come under deceptive practices.

### 3.4.2 Offensive Materials and Objectionable Business Development Practices

The marketers control what they say to customers as well as and how and where they say it. When events, television or radio programming, or publications sponsored by a marketer, in addition to products or promotional materials, are perceived as offensive, they often create strong negative reactions.

For example, some people find advertising for all products promoting sexual potency to be offensive. Others may be offended when a promotion employs stereotypical images or uses sex as an appeal. This is particularly true when a product is being marketed in other countries, where words and images may assume different meanings than they do in the host country.

When people feel that products or appeals are offensive, they may pressure vendors to stop carrying the product. Thus, all promotional messages must be carefully screened and tested, and communication media, programming, and editorial content selected to match the tastes and interests of targeted customers. Beyond the target audience, however, the marketers should understand that there are others who are not customers might also receive their appeals and see their images and be offended.

Direct marketing is also undergoing closer examination. Objectionable practices range from minor irritants, such as, the timing and frequency of sales letters or commercials, to those that are offensive or even illegal. Among the examples of practices that may raise ethical questions are persistent and high-pressure selling, annoying telemarketing calls, and television commercials that are too long or run too frequently.

Business development appeals created to take advantage of young or inexperienced consumers or senior citizens – including advertisements, sales appeals disguised as contests, junk mail (including electronic mail), and the use and exchange of mailing lists—may also pose ethical questions. In addition to being subject to consumer protection laws and regulations, the Direct Marketing Association provides a list of voluntary ethical guidelines for companies engaged in direct marketing.

### 3.4.3 Ethical Product and Distribution Practices

Several product-related issues raise questions about ethics in business development, most often concerning the quality of products and services provided. Among the most frequently voiced complaints are ones about products that are unsafe, that are of poor quality in construction or content, that do not contain what is promoted, or that go out of style or become obsolete before they actually need replacing.

An organisation that markets poor quality or unsafe products resorts to a serious gamble since, in the long run, they will earn a reputation for poor products or service. In addition, it may be putting itself in jeopardy for product claims or legal action. Sometimes, however, frequent changes in product features or performance, such as, those that often occur in the computer industry, make previous models of products obsolete. Such changes can be misinterpreted as planned obsolescence.

Ethical questions may also arise in the distribution process. Since sales performance is the barometer that help measure the performance of the marketing representatives and sales personnel; invariably performance pressures often fuel unethical practices and thereby raise ethical dilemmas.

For example, pressuring vendors to buy more than what they require and pushing items that will result in higher commissions are temptations. That apart, exerting influence to cause vendors to reduce display space for competitors' products, promising shipment when knowing delivery is not possible by the promised date, or paying vendors to carry a firm's product rather than one of its competitors are also unethical.

Research is another area in which ethical issues may arise. Information gathered from research can be important to the successful marketing of products or services. Consumers, however, may view the organisations' efforts to gather data from them as being intrusive. They are resistant to give out personal information that might cause them to become a business development target or to receive product or sales information. When data about products or consumers are exaggerated to make a selling point, or research questions are written to obtain a specific result, consumers are misled. Without self-imposed ethical standards in the research process, the management will in all likelihood make decisions based on inaccurate information.

### 3.4.4 Does Business Development Overfocus on Materialism?

The consumers develop an identity in the marketplace that is shaped both by who they are and by what they see themselves as becoming. There is evidence that the way consumers view themselves influences their purchasing behaviour. This identity is often reflected in the brands or products they consume or the way in which they lead their lives.

The proliferation of information about products and services complicates decision-making. Sometimes, the consumer desires to achieve or maintain a certain lifestyle or image which results in their purchasing more than they actually need or can afford.

Does marketing create these wants? Clearly, appeals exist that are designed to cause people to purchase more than they need or can afford. Unsolicited offers of credit cards with high limits or high interest rates, advertising appeals touting the psychological benefits of conspicuous consumption, and promotions that seek to stimulate unrecognised needs are often cited as examples of these excesses.

### 3.4.5 Special Ethical Issues in Marketing to Children

The children too constitute an important marketing target for certain products. Because their knowledge about products, the media, and selling strategies is usually not as well developed as that of adults, they are likely to be more vulnerable to psychological appeals and strong images. Thus, ethical questions sometimes arise when they are exposed to questionable business development tactics and messages. For example, studies linking relationships between tobacco and alcohol business development with youth consumption resulted in increased public pressure directly leading to the regulation of marketing for those products.

The proliferation of direct marketing and use of the Internet to market to children also raises ethical issues. Sometimes, a few unscrupulous marketers design sites so that children are able to bypass adult supervision or control. At times, they present objectionable materials to underage consumers or pressure them to buy items or provide credit card numbers. When this happens, it is likely that social pressure and subsequent regulation will result. Likewise, programming for children and youth in the mass media has been under scrutiny for many years.

In many countries, marketing to children is closely controlled. The Federal regulations place limits on the types of marketing that can be directed to children, and marketing activities are monitored by the government, consumer and parental groups, and the broadcast networks. These guidelines provide clear direction to marketers.

### 3.4.6 Ethical Issues in Business Development to Minorities

The United States is a society of ever-increasing diversity, wherein markets are broken into segments in which people share some similar characteristics. Ethical issues arise when business development tactics are designed specifically to exploit or manipulate a minority market segment. Offensive practices may take the form of negative or stereotypical representations of minorities, associating the consumption of harmful or questionable products with a particular minority segment, and demeaning portrayals of a race or group. Ethical questions may also arise when high-pressure selling is directed at a group, when higher prices are charged for products sold to minorities, or even when stores provide poorer service in neighbourhoods with a high population of minority customers. Such practices will likely result in a bad public image and lost sales for the marketer.

Unlike the legal protections in place to protect children from harmful practices, there have been few efforts to protect minority customers. When targeting minorities, the firms concerned must evaluate whether the targeted population is susceptible to appeals because of their minority status. The firm must assess business development efforts to determine whether ethical behaviour would cause them to change their marketing practices.

### 3.4.7 Ethical Issues Surrounding the Portrayal of Women in Business Development Efforts

As society changes, so do the images of and roles assumed by people, regardless of race, sex, or occupation. Over the years, the women have been portrayed in a variety of ways. When marketers present those images as overly conventional, formulaic, or oversimplified, people may view them as stereotypical and offensive.

Examples of demeaning stereotypes include those in which women are presented as less intelligent, submissive to or obsessed with men, unable to assume leadership roles or make decisions, or skimpily dressed in order to appeal to the sexual interests of males. Harmful stereotypes include, those portraying women as obsessed with their appearance or conforming to some ideal of size, weight, or beauty. When images are considered demeaning or harmful, they will work to the detriment of the organisation. Advertisements, in particular, should be evaluated to be sure that the images projected are not offensive.

Since business development decisions often require specialised knowledge, ethical issues are often more complicated than those faced in personal life and effective decision-making requires consistency. As each business situation is different, and not all decisions are simple, many organisations have embraced ethical codes of conduct and rules of professional ethics to guide managers and employees. However, sometimes self-regulation proves insufficient to protect the interest of customers, organisations, or society. At that point, pressures for regulation and enactment of legislation to protect the interests of all parties in the exchange process will likely occur.

## 3.5 Developing Business Ethics in a Global Economy

Globalisation has brought about greater involvement with ethical considerations and, more importantly, for attaining competitive edge through practising business ethics. Globalisation and business ethics are linked as they affect a company's ability to commit to its shareholders, in particular, to external investors, and preserve the trust needed for further investment and growth.

It is increasingly important for companies to deal with ethics as a corporate strategy that, if uniquely implemented, could achieve competitive advantage for a given company rather than having to wait for reacting to possible ethical issues of importance to the targeted stakeholders. It is any day better to be an ethically proactive company rather than being a ethically reactive company.

As the speed of comparable tangible assets acquisition accelerates and the pace of imitation quickens, the firms that want to sustain distinctive global competitive advantages need to protect, exploit and enhance their unique intangible assets, particularly, integrity (building firms of integrity is the hidden logic of business ethics). Sustainable global competitive advantage occurs when a company implements a value-creating strategy which other companies are unable to imitate. For example, a company with superior business leadership skills in enhancing integrity capacity increases its reputation capital with multiple stakeholders and thereby positions itself way ahead of its immediate competitors.

Aiming at justifying their decisions relative to ethics, the individuals concerned resort to moral philosophies –principles or rules that each one uses when deciding what is right or wrong:

- Globalisation has brought about greater involvement with ethical considerations and, more importantly, for attaining competitive edge through practising business ethics.
- Globalisation and business ethics are linked as they affect a company's ability to commit to its shareholders, in particular, to external investors, and preserve the trust needed for further investment and growth.
- It is increasingly important for companies to deal with ethics as a corporate strategy that, if uniquely implemented, could achieve competitive advantage for a given company rather than having to wait for reacting to possible ethical issues of importance to the targeted stakeholders.
- It is any day better to be an ethically proactive company rather than being a ethically reactive company.
- As the speed of comparable tangible assets acquisition accelerates and the pace of imitation quickens, the firms that want to sustain distinctive global competitive advantages need to protect, exploit and enhance their unique intangible assets, particularly, integrity (building firms of integrity is the hidden logic of business ethics).
- Sustainable global competitive advantage occurs when a company implements a value-creating strategy which other companies are unable to imitate.
- For example, a company with superior business leadership skills in enhancing integrity capacity increases its reputation capital with multiple stakeholders and thereby positions itself way ahead of its immediate competitors.

Although it appears there is a genuine opportunity to improve the standards of business ethics across the globe, it should not be forgotten that unethical business practices are not restricted to any particular country or culture. There would always be around some individuals who will put personal gain ahead of ethical practice; think Enron, Arthur Anderson, WorldCom, Barings Bank and, most recently, Societe Generale. A global economy will operate regardless of the ethical environment, and there is at least as much opportunity for promoting unethical practice as there is for effecting changes for the better.

### 3.5.1 Global Ethical Issues

When we talk about ethics or CSR in the context of international business, there is a view that the managers/companies should not bother too much about the varying norms of morality in the host country; they should, in fact, go ahead and implement their home country norms.

1. **Absolutism vs. Relativism**
   - Absolutism ( When in Rome or anywhere else, do as you would at home)
   - Relativism ( When in Rome, do as Romans do)

   In absolutism, the business ought to be conducted in the same way across the world with a single code of conduct in their dealings everywhere; whereas in relativism, the only guide for business conduct abroad is what is legally and morally accepted in the country where it operates.

   It would be relevant to mention some of the sensitive and controversial ethical issues in the International business or market.

2. **Bribery and Corruption**

   Bribery is a deliberate attempt to persuade someone (usually in position of power and authority) to act improperly in favour of the briber. The briber usually does so by offering money or gifts or any other inducements to the aforesaid person in authority in lieu of obtaining favour. Corruption is understood as the abuse of public property for private gain. In international business, bribery and corrupt practices are used to gain an unfair advantage over its rivals and exercising its monopoly. Even though there are good provisions to watch all these illegal and unethical practices like, the OECD countries strict norms for taxing, USA's Foreign Corrrupt Practices Act etc. these issues nevertheless still persist.

3. **Ethics and Human Rights**

   The issue is related to whether or not an international firm should move to a country where human rights are found violated. The other view is that economic prosperity and political freedom go hand in hand. If foreign trade and investment bring about improvement in the living standards, human rights abuses could be contained.

4. **Ethics and Consumerism**

   The consumer protection activities are more practised in developed countries than in developing countries. Further, ethical issues unique to MNCs arose from the diversity of national operating locations set against the uniformity of the multinational organisations (Tavis, 1996). This scenario gave leeway for MNCs to act in an egocentric manner, in part, because of a lack of any other uniform set of standards to apply across multiple cultures and operating situations. As a result, many MNCs started acting as if they were "law unto themselves" and were found to be selling harmful products in emerging economics.

### 5. Safety and Environmental Issues

Safety and enironmental issues are very sensitive one in the international market. One finds that Safety and Environmental laws are very strict in western countries. If those rules will be followed in the developing countries, the cost of production will go up and thereby the competitive strength along with the local manufacturers will be seriously eroded. If they are not followed, it goes against the ethical norms of the given Multinational Corporation.

## 3.5.2 Global Institutes Providing Help in Ethical Implementation

The International support for ethics and its implementation across the globe can be seen by the following institutions which support and guide to follow the same:

### 1. ECS2000:

The Ethics Compliance Management System Standard (ECS2000) is a guideline for corporations and other organisations which are endeavouring to conduct business in an equitable and responsible manner. The ECS2000 standard has been made publicly available by the Business Ethics Research Project at the Reitaku Centre for Economic Research. It is a very useful document for any organisation which aim to establish, apply, maintain and consistently improve an ethical-legal compliance management system.

### 2. Caux Round Table:

The Caux Round Table (CRT) is an international network of principled business leaders working to promote moral capitalism. The CRT advocates the implementation of the CRT principles for business through which principled capitalism can flourish and sustainable and socially responsible prosperity can become the foundation for a free, fair and transparent global society.

### 3. Canadian Business for Social Responsibility:

The Canadian Business for Social Responsibility (CBSR) is a non-profit, business-led, national membership organisation of Canadian companies working to improve their social, environmental and financial performance. They have developed the GoodCompany Guidelines for Corporate Social Performance which are a set of guidelines that outline what companies can do to become more socially and environmentally responsible.

### 4. E-Ethics Centre:

The e-business ethics centre from the University of Colorado provides a source of information on business ethics, corporate citizenship and organisational compliance. The goal of the e-business ethics centre is to create a virtual community of organisations and individuals that share best practices in the improvement of business ethics.

### 5. Business for Social Responsibility:

Business for Social Responsibility (BSR) is a global organisation that helps member companies achieve success in ways that respect ethical values, people, communities and the environment. BSR provides information, tools, training and advisory services to make corporate social responsibility an integral part of business operations and strategies.

6. **OECD Principles of Corporate Governance:**

The OECD Principles of Corporate Governance were endorsed by OECD Ministers in 1999 and revised in 2004. They cover six key areas of corporate governance, namely - ensuring the basis for an effective corporate governance framework; the rights of shareholders; the equitable treatment of shareholders; the role of stakeholders in corporate governance; disclosure and transparency; and the responsibilities of the board.

7. **Transparency International:**

Transparency International is an international non-governmental organisation which brings civil society, business, and governments together in a powerful global coalition, and works at both the national and international level to curb both the supply and demand of corruption.

8. **European Corporate Governance Institute:**

The European Corporate Governance Institute (ECGI) is an international scientific non-profit association which provides a forum for debate and dialogue between academics, legislators and practitioners, focusing on major corporate governance issues and thereby promoting best practice.

9. **International Business Ethics Institute:**

The International Business Ethics Institute promotes business ethics and corporate responsibility through two key programme areas. First, it works to increase public awareness and dialogue about international business ethics issues through such educational resources and activities, as the, Round Table Discussion Series, the International Business Ethics Review and their website. Second, the Institute works closely with companies to assist them in establishing effective international ethics programmes.

10. **Global Compact:**

The Global Compact is an international initiative that will bring companies together with UN agencies, labour and civil society to support nine (now ten) principles in the areas of human rights, labour, the environment, and anti-corruption. It seeks to advance responsible corporate citizenship so that business can be part of the solution to the challenges of globalisation.

### 3.5.3 Guidelines to Ensure Code of Ethics for Global Business

Unfortunately, the idea that business ethics is good business is not uniformly agreed upon around the world. Western nations have formalised ethics programmmes due to regulatory initiatives, corporate scandals, and increasing public scrutiny. The corporations in western nations already have codes of conduct or full-fledged ethics programmes and understand the business case for evaluating right vs. wrong in business. In developing countries, the businesses are beginning to acknowledge the incentives for ethical decision-making. However, business ethics has not translated into common practice due to moral expectations and all-pervasive corruption.

The international differences in ethics poses significant challenges as businesses expand and move into new regions. One problem arises as western corporations expand into developing countries, where ethical corporate decision-making is not the norm. This directional flow is the most traditional and prevalent path businesses take. As far back as the 17th century, the English East India country engaged in trade with territories in India to as far east as Japan. A more recent example is the Ford Motor Company, which opened its first dealerships in China in 1993.

Another problem arises when companies originate in a 'business is business' environment and spread to countries where business ethics is expected and legally necessary. The second directional flow describes a non-western corporation spreading to western, developed nations. The Toyota Motor Company is a successful example of this less common recent trend. These two directional flows highlight the disparity in business ethics abroad. As businesses move from one landscape to another, they must first understand business ethics in their new environment.

In order to address how global companies can preserve ethics in an increasingly flat world, let us set up a hypothetical situation. Since space is limited, the example will demonstrate the more common directional flow. If Japanese Company chooses to open a new office in Brazil, a country where ethical decision-making is not integrated into business practice, they will be faced with the challenge of translating its current ethics programme into the new landscape. While there is no uniform solution, the following framework is helpful in addressing business ethics in a flat world. The overall message is that ethics codes must be guided by clear principles tailored to local needs in an explicit code.

1. **Perform an Ethics-focused Evaluation of the Environment:** In the aforesaid scenario, the Japanese company must first try and understand the trends that shape their specific industry and environment. The Company must then ask questions, such as: How is business ethics viewed in Brazil? Are there advisory or mandatory regulations for ethics programmes? How do external and internal stakeholders view corporate social responsibility?

2. **Tailor Ethics Programme to the Local Environment:** The Japanese Company must mould its message and means of delivering the message to the local environment. Questions to ask include: What message will garner the most buy-in from employees? Does the message address key issues and risks of the company and local context? What type of communication methods will be most effective in this setting?

3. **Engage the Support of Top-level Management:** The top-level management must be the greatest proponents of the ethic programmes. Their support sets an example for the entire organisation.
4. **Appoint an Ethics Officer:** Designating a position to guide the company's business ethics signals the importance of ethics to the organisation. The ethics officer communicates the ethics message and is responsible for keeping the company accountable.
5. **Reinforce Ethics Code with Constant Training for all Employees:** Ethics training should permeate all employee levels and occur in regular monthly/annual intervals. This signals that ethics is a company-wide and permanent initiative.

## 3.6 Marketing Ethics in Foreign Trade

Marketing ethics are the basic principles and values that govern the business practices of those engaged in promoting products or services to consumers. Marketing ethics is a part of business ethics in the sense that marketing forms a significant part of any business model.

Due to the globalisation of markets and production, ever increasing number of foreign trade personnel have to deal with ethical issues in cross-cultural settings. Murphy and Laczniak asserted two decades ago that "as more firms move into multinational marketing, ethical issues tend to increase".

In a cross-cultural environment, marketers are exposed to different values and ethical norms. Which ethical position should marketers take when acting in a foreign culture? The important question to be answered in foreign trade is whose ethics does the marketer use?

A marketer cannot leave his ethics behind as he ventures around the globe. In foreign trade and international marketing, the ethical decision-making process can be influenced by many ethical approaches.

The moral question of what is right or appropriate poses many dilemmas for marketing and marketers domestically. Even within a country, ethical standards are frequently not defined or always clear. The problem of ethics is considerably more complex in the international marketplace, because value judgements differ widely among culturally diverse groups. That which is commonly accepted as right on one country may be completely unacceptable in another. Giving business gifts of high value, for example, is generally condemned in the United States, but in many countries of the world gifts are not only accepted but also expected.

Upon examination of existing ethical frameworks in the field of international marketing and foreign trade, it is argued that marketers cannot always rely on universally accepted ethical norms, such as hyper norms or core values that have been suggested by a deluge of marketing literature. Some basic moral values could be used in evaluating international marketing ethical issues.

Violations of basic moral values in international marketing settings should be accepted as ethical problems. After studying the literature related to international marketing, it is easily seen that most of the marketing ethics studies involve the use of scenarios as research instruments and relate to the following marketing sub-disciplines market research, retail management, purchasing management, advertising management, marketing management, industrial marketing, and marketing education.

## 3.7 Role of Business Ethics in Developing a Civilised Society

Is there a difference between business ethics and social responsibility? Are the two mutually compatible or mutually exclusive? It is clearly impossible to do a one-on-one comparison between ethical standards and social responsibility principles if, for no other reason, than there are twelve ethical standards and seven principles for social responsibility. Nevertheless, a side-by-side look at the standards and principles provides the opportunity to make some initial comparisons and begin to question their compatibility or mutual exclusivity :

### Table 3.2 : Ethical Standards and Social Responsibility Principles

| Ethical Standards | Social Responsibility Principles |
|---|---|
| Perceived impropriety | Community |
| Responsibilities to the employer | Diversity |
| Conflict of interest | Environment |
| Issues of influence | Ethics |
| Confidential and proprietary information | Financial responsibility |
| Supplier relationships | Human rights |
| Reciprocity | Safety |
| Applicable laws | |
| Small, disadvantages and minority-owned businesses | |
| Professional competence | |
| National international supply management conduct | |
| Responsibilities to the profession | |

The buying organisations have the ability to influence and/or demand both ethical behaviour and social responsibility from their suppliers, but should they? When it comes to ethics, an implicit agreement of longstanding exists that ethical behaviour is not only desirable but required in domestic business transactions. Any debate stems from doing business globally wherein the ethics standard recommends being "especially sensitive to customs and cultural differences with respect to social and business behaviour and issues of influence."

Influencing or demanding social responsibility from suppliers has no such caveat and poses such questions as :

- Is it ethical to influence the social responsibility of suppliers?
- Is it ethical to demand, by way of contract language, socially responsible behaviour from suppliers?

Perhaps, the first thing that becomes apparent in comparing the ethics standards and the social responsibility principles is that 'ethics' are firmly embedded in the social responsibility principles.

The ethical standard for small, disadvantaged and minority-owned businesses seems to relate to the social responsibility principle of diversity. The commentary for the ethical standard, "encourage, support for small, disadvantaged and minority-owned businesses," recommends specific activities to stimulate growth in this segment of the supply base. The social responsibility principle includes:

1. Proactively promote purchasing from, and the development of, socially diverse suppliers.
2. Encourage diversity within your own organisation.
3. Proactively promote diverse employment practices throughout the supply chain.

Since the social responsibility principle is much broader than the ethical standard, a direct relationship is not as well defined as that concerning ethics and questions begin to emerge. Many organisations donate to community organisations and have developed written policies encouraging employees to volunteer in community service. The principle, however, demands going beyond the boundaries of one's own organisation and encouraging the members of the supply chain to add value in their communities. To meet this principle, the organisations should:

1. Develop statements reflecting their tenets that community support is a good idea.
2. Demand that suppliers adhere to the buying organisation's written policies.
3. Require suppliers to have their own policies and programmes supporting their communities.
4. Request that suppliers donate to community organisations.
5. Set goals and mandate that suppliers volunteer in community service to meet these goals.

The social responsibility principle on human rights provides fertile ground for debate and is described as follows:
1. Treat people with dignity and respect.
2. Support and respect the protection of international human rights within the organisation's sphere of influence.
3. Encourage your own organisation and its supply chains to avoid complicity in human or employment rights abuses.

While there may be no argument regarding the compatibility between ethical standards and social responsibility principles regarding supporting and respecting human rights and treating people with dignity and respect, how far does an organisation go in encouraging its supply chains to avoid complicity in human or employment rights abuses?

Ethical values are the foundation on which a civilised society exists. Devoid of this foundation, civilisation collapses. Real business ethics is a natural and important element of any serious business strategy. Ethics involves treating people – customers, employees, shareholders, suppliers, with fairness, consideration and respect while providing goods and services that helps in acheiving customer's needs and expectations.

Quite simply, ethical practices are people-oriented ways of doing business. The businesses that prosper will be those that hold fast to this thread by keeping people at the top of their agenda. After all, ethics is one topic that begins and ends with people.

While discussing the role of Business Ethics in building a good society, we need to consider it from the different perspectives that drive a good society. They are as follows :

### 3.7.1 Environmental Perspectives

The environmental perspective emerged from forestry management and, then later, in other areas of resource management.

The basic principles of the environmental perspective concern the effective management of physical resources so that they are conserved for the future. All bio-systems are regarded as having finite resources and finite capacity, and hence, a business activity must operate at a level that does not threaten the health of those systems.

Even at the most basic level, these concerns suggest a need to address a number of critical business problems, such as, the impacts of industrialisation on biodiversity, the continued use of non-renewable resources such as, oil, steel, and coal, as well as the production of damaging environmental pollutants like greenhouse gases and CFCs from industrial plants and consumer products.

At a more fundamental level though, these concerns also raise the problem of economic growth itself, and the important question of whether future generations can really enjoy the current living standards without a reversal of the trend towards ever more production and consumption.

## 3.7.2 Economic Perspectives

The economic perspective initially emerged from economic growth models that assessed the limits imposed by the carrying capacity of the earth. The recognition that continued growth in population, industrial activity, resource use, and pollution could mean that standards of living would eventually decline, led to the emergence of sustainability as a way of thinking about ensuring that future generations would not be adversely disadvantaged by the activities and choices of the present generation.

Economists such as Kenneth Arrow (Arrow and Hurwicz 1977), Herman Daly (Daly 1991; Daly and Cobb 1989), and David Pearce (1999) have since been highly influential in advancing the agenda for macroeconomic understanding of business ethics.

The implications for business ethics of such thinking occur on different levels. A narrow concept of economic sustainability focuses on the economic performance of the corporation itself: the responsibility of management is to develop, produce, and market those products that secure the long-term economic performance for the corporation in question. This includes a focus on those strategies which, for example, lead to a long-term rise in share price, revenues and market share rather than short-term 'explosions' of profits at the expense of long-term viability of success.

A broader view of this concept would include the company's attitude towards and impacts upon the economic framework in which it is embedded. Paying bribes or building cartels, for instance, could be regarded as economically unethical because these activities undermine the long-term functioning of markets.

The corporations which attempt to avoid paying corporate taxes through subtle accounting manipulations might be said to behave in an unethical way : if they are not willing to fund the political, institutional environment (such as, schools, hospitals, the police, and the justice system) they erode one of the key institutional bases of their corporate success. The international pressure group, the Tax Justice Network, has therefore, formed a coalition of researchers and activists with a shared concern about such issues to raise awareness and stimulate action against the harmful impacts of tax avoidance, tax competition, and tax havens.

## 3.7.3 Social Perspectives

The development of the social perspective on the global economy has tended to lag behind that of the environmental and economic perspectives and remains a relatively new development.

The explicit integration of social concerns into the business discourse around ethics can be seen to have emerged during the 1990s, in response to concerns regarding the impacts of business activities on indigenous communities in less developed countries and regions. It would therefore be wrong to assume though that this means that, until this time, local community claims on business (and other social issues) went entirely unheard by business, or unexamined by business ethics scholars.

The key issue in the social perspective on ethics is that of social justice. Social responsibility, in this context, means that business must:

(a) Accommodate itself to social change if it is expected to survive;
(b) Take a long-run enlightened view of self-interest and help to solve social problems in order to create a better environment for itself;
(c) Discharge its moral obligation to help solve social problems that it had created or perpetrated;
(c) Try to pre-empt government regulation by meeting social expectations before they become politicised and invite governmental intervention;
(e) Apply its enormous resources (built out of societal contributions) to solve social problems;
(f) Use the social problems as profitable business opportunities as their service to society; and
(g) Attempt to gain a better public image by being socially responsible.

## Points to Remember

1. **Globalisation** is the progressive eroding of the relevance of territorial bases for social, economic and political activities, processes and relations.
2. **Issues in global business ethics perspective**
    - Cultural Issues
    - Legal Issues
    - Accountability Issues
3. **Areas of concern in business development ethics**
    - Unfair or deceptive business development practices
    - Offensive materials and objectionable business development practices
    - Ethical Product and Distribution Practices
    - Does Business Development Overfocus on Materialism
    - Special Ethical Issues in Marketing to Children
    - Ethical Issues in Business Development to Minorities
    - Ethical Issues Surrounding the Portrayal of Women in Business Development Efforts
4. **Global Ethical Issues**
    - Absolutism vs. Relativism
    - Bribery and Corruption
    - Ethics and Human Rights

- Ethics and Consumerism
- Safety and Environmental Issues

5. **Global Institutes Providing Help in Ethical Implementation**
    - ECS2000
    - Caux Round Table
    - Canadian Business for Social Responsibility
    - E-Ethics Centre
    - Business for Social Responsibility
    - OECD Principles of Corporate Governance
    - Transparency International
    - European Corporate Governance Institute
    - International Business Ethics Institute
    - Global Compact

6. **Guidelines to Ensure code of ethics for global Business**
    - Perform an Ethics-focused Evaluation of the Environment
    - Tailor Ethics Programme to the Local Environment
    - Engage the Support of Top-level Management
    - Appoint an Ethics Officer
    - Reinforce Ethics Code with Constant Training for all Employees

7. While discussing the role of Business Ethics in building a good society, we need to consider it from the different perspectives that drive a good society. They are as follows:
    - Environmental perspectives
    - Economic perspectives
    - Social perspectives

## Questions for Discussion

1. Write a note on Globalisation. What is its impact in the Indian context?
2. What are the main issues to be looked at from the business ethics perspective in global business environment?
3. Describe the three perspectives that drive a good society.
4. Discuss the relationship among business, business ethics and business development.
5. What are the issues of concern in developing global business ethics?

# Chapter 4...
# Moral Issues in Business

## Contents ...

- 4.1 Introduction
- 4.2 Concept of Corporate Social Responsibility (CSR)
    - 4.2.1 Importance of Corporate Social Responsibility
    - 4.2.2 Responsibility towards Different Interest Groups
    - 4.2.3 Relationship between Corporate Social Responsibility and Business Ethics
    - 4.2.4 Arguments for Corporate Social Responsibility
    - 4.2.5 Arguments against Corporate Social Responsibility
- 4.3 Justice and Economic System Ethics
- 4.4 Business Ethics and Environment Protection : Ethics relating to Environment Protection
    - 4.4.1 Concern for Future Generation
    - 4.4.2 Polluting Activities
    - 4.4.3 Human Interest and Eco-System
    - 4.4.4 Environmental Ethics
    - 4.4.5 Survey of Polluting Practices
    - 4.4.6 Ethical Responsibility
    - 4.4.7 Disposal of Waste
    - 4.4.8 Socio-Political Dimension of Pollution Control
- 4.5 Business Ethics and Consumer Protection
    - 4.5.1 Problems Faced by Consumers
    - 4.5.2 Legal Protection to Consumers
    - 4.5.3 Business Obligation towards Consumer Protection
- 4.6 Business Ethics and Social Justice
- 4.7 Role of Social Responsibility in Indian Companies
- Points to Remember
- Questions for Discussion

## Learning Objectives ...

- ➢ To gain knowledge of the concept of Corporate Social Responsibility
- ➢ To explore the relationship between CSR and Business Ethics
- ➢ To be able to argue for and against CSR
- ➢ To learn about business ethics in the areas of environment protection, consumer protection and social justice

## 4.1 Introduction

Ethics is not easy for any business, and there will always be individuals and/or groups who question the behaviour of institutions in various systems in society, be it - the justice, the economic or any other system. Ethics and social responsibility are the concern of every one, and it is up to the individuals concerned to establish ethical codes and follow them.

Early writings on ethics were centred not on economics or business, but personal beliefs and actions. It becomes readily apparent from early discussions of ethics that philosophers and writers viewed ethics as a matter of choice. Individuals must make choices in their lives.

This is important to note – businesses do not make choices. Choices are made and/or implemented by individuals within the justice or economic enterprise. People in government make choices, people in educational institutions make choices, people in businesses make choices, people with churches make choices; everyone is forced to make choices, and even the choice not to choose is a *choice*, in itself.

Closely related to ethical codes are responsibilities that economic enterprises have to society. This is known as social responsibility. This is a difficult element of business operations because it normally means additional costs to the business.

Social responsibility could mean making contributions to charitable organisations. An example might be a corporation donating land it is not using to a conservation group for the development of a nature preserve or a sanctuary.

Social responsibility also includes internal considerations, such as, hiring minorities, establishing on-site child-care facilities, controlling pollution, ensuring safe working conditions, providing substance-abuse programmes for employees, and manufacturing safe products. These are all economic decisions that have social effects both within and outside the business.

Businesses that are concerned about social responsibility will conduct social audits. This is a systematic evaluation of the organisation's progress toward implementing socially responsible programmes. This is not a precise science and depends on the interpretations of what is socially responsive behaviour. Again, these decisions must be made by individuals within the business. Social audits do illustrate that a business is at least concerned about the social impact it has.

## 4.2 Concept of Corporate Social Responsibility (CSR)

We all know that people engage in business to earn profit. However, profit-making is not the sole function of business. It performs a number of social functions, as it is a part of the society. It takes care of those who are instrumental in securing its existence and survival like, the owners, investors, employees, consumers and government, in particular, and the society and community, in general. Therefore, every business ought to contribute in some way or the other for their benefit. For example, every business must ensure a satisfactory rate of return to investors, provide good salary, security and proper working condition to its employees, make available quality products at reasonable price to its consumers, maintain the environment properly etc.

However, while doing so two things need to be noted to view it as corporate social responsibility or social responsibility of business. First, any such activity is not charity. It means that if any business donates some amount of money to any hospital or temple or school and college etc., it is not to be considered as discharge of social responsibility because charity does not imply fulfilling responsibility.

Secondly, any such activity should not be such that it is good for somebody and bad for others. Suppose a businessman makes a lot of money by smuggling or by cheating customers, and then, runs a hospital to treat poor patients at low prices, his actions cannot be socially justified. Social responsibility implies that a businessman should not do anything harmful to the society in course of his business activities.

The obligation of any business to protect and serve public interest is known as corporate social responsibility. Thus, the concept of social responsibility discourages businessmen from adopting unfair means like, black marketing, hoarding, adulteration, tax evasion and cheating customers etc., in order to earn profit. Instead, it encourages them to earn profit through judicious management of the business, by providing better working and living conditions to its employees, providing better products, after sales service etc., to its customers and simultaneously control pollution and conserve natural resources.

- *"Corporate social responsibility refers to the obligations of businessmen to pursue those policies, to make those decisions, or to follow those lines of action, which are desirable in terms of objectives and values of society."*   **Bowen**
- *"Corporate social responsibility are the actions that appear to further some social good, beyond the interest of the firm and that which is required by law."*   **McWilliams**
- *"The social responsibility of business encompasses the economic, legal, ethical and discretionary expectations that society has of organisations at a given point in time."* **Carroll**

### 4.2.1 Importance of Corporate Social Responsibility

Social responsibility is a voluntary effort on the part of business to take various steps to satisfy the expectation of the different interest groups. As you have already learnt, the interest groups may be - owners, investors, employees, consumers, government and society or community. But the question arises as to why should the business come forward and be responsible towards these interest groups? Let us consider the following points:

(a) **Public Image:** The activities of business towards the welfare of the society earn goodwill and reputation for the business. The earnings of business also depend upon the public image of its activities. People will any day prefer to buy products of a company that engages itself in various social welfare programmes. Again, good public image also attracts honest and competent employees to work with such employers.

(b) **Government Regulation:** To avoid government regulations, businessmen should discharge their duties voluntarily. For example, if any business firm pollutes the environment, it will naturally come under strict government regulation, which may ultimately force the firm to close down its business. Instead, the business firm should engage itself in maintaining a pollution-free environment.

(c) **Survival and Growth:** Every business is a part of the society. So for its survival and growth, support from the society is very much essential. Since any given business utilises the available resources like power, water, land, roads, etc., of the society, it should be the responsibility of every business to spend a part of its profit for the welfare of the society.

(d) **Employee Satisfaction:** Besides getting good salary and working in a healthy atmosphere, employees also expect other facilities like, proper accommodation, transportation, education and training. The employers should try to fulfill all the expectation of the employees because employee satisfaction is directly related to productivity and it is also required for the long-term prosperity of the organisation. For example, if business spends money on training of the employees, it will have more efficient people to work and, thereby, earn more profit.

(e) **Consumer Awareness:** Nowadays consumers have become very conscious about their rights. They protest against the supply of inferior and harmful products by forming different groups. This has made it obligatory for the business to protect the interests of the consumers by providing quality products at the most competitive price.

## 4.2.2 Responsibility towards Different Interest Groups

After getting some idea about the concept and importance of social responsibility of business, let us look into the various responsibilities that a business has towards different groups with whom it interacts. The business generally interacts with owners, investors, employees, suppliers, customers, competitors, government and society. They are called as interest groups because by each and every activity of business, the interest of these groups is affected directly or indirectly.

1. **Responsibility towards Owners:** The owners are the persons who own the business. They contribute capital and bear the business risks. The primary responsibilities of a business towards its owners are to -

    (a) Run the business efficiently;

    (b) Proper utilisation of capital and other resources;

    (c) Growth and appreciation of capital; and

    (d) Regular and fair return on capital invested.

2. **Responsibility towards Investors:** Investors are those who provide finance by way of investment in debentures, bonds, deposits etc. Also, banks, financial institutions, and investing public are all included in this category. The responsibilities of a business towards its investors are:

    (a) Ensuring safety of their investment;

    (b) Regular payment of interest; and

    (c) Timely repayment of principal amount.

3. **Responsibility towards Employees:** A business needs employees or workers to work for it. These employees put their best efforts for the benefit of the given business. Therefore, it becomes the prime responsibility of every business to take care of the interest of their employees. If the employees are satisfied and efficient, then, and only then, can a business be successful. The responsibilities of a business towards its employees, includes:

    (i) **Wages and Taxes:** You have a responsibility to pay employees of your small business at least the minimum hourly wage in your state and to pay each employee money owed from working per pay period, including overtime, sick leave and vacation wages. Paychecks should always be on time and without delay so your workers can meet individual financial obligations. The IRS and state government also requires you to pay Medicare, Social Security, state and federal taxes out of employee wages for each employee working for your small business.

    (ii) **Workplace Safety Standards:** The government requires you to maintain a safe working environment for your employees as per the standards for your small business's industry set forth by the Occupational Safety and Health Administration. You must also make employees aware of areas in your business that have a high risk for injury and train your employees in safety procedures to minimise the risk of injury. Ensuring each employee is using tools and equipment safe for your small business's particular industry is also your responsibility as a business owner. Continual inspection of your facilities and employee knowledge of safety standards is necessary to make certain your workplace remains as safe as possible.

(iii) **Workers' Compensation Insurance:** Despite your best efforts to maintain a safe working environment, accidents will happen. When injuries occur through no fault of your employees, it's your responsibility to file a claim with your workers' compensation insurance provider. This coverage provides for medical care and wage replacement for your injured employee. You must treat your injured employee with respect and file the claim without attempting to cause a delay in processing or attempt to deter the worker from filing a claim at all. This is illegal and can cost you hefty fines and possible jail time if you refuse to honour your commitment and requirements as a business owner.

(iv) **Positive Working Climate:** Employees of your small business don't have to be cheery, but the environment shouldn't encourage workers to harass each other in any way. It is your responsibility as a small business owner to create a working climate that fosters respect and fair treatment of every employee regardless of age, race, gender, ethnicity, country of origin, disability or religion. Never ignore employees who come to you with problems of harassment. Confronting these issues directly can help you avoid a costly civil lawsuit from allowing a climate of harassment in your workplace.

4. **Responsibility towards Suppliers:** Suppliers are businessmen who supply raw materials and other items required by the manufacturers and traders. Certain suppliers, called distributors, supply finished products to the consumers. The responsibilities of business towards these suppliers are:

(i) **Human Rights:** The business community, including organisations dealing with contractors and suppliers, has the responsibility to uphold human rights. This means that they should not in any way infringe human rights. Specifically, business operations often tend to be a point of contention where human rights may be negatively influenced or positively enforced. Businesses operating within or outside the country should be able to promote the rule of law. For instance, if they are dealing with contractors working in less favourable environments, they should be able to offer or at least ensure that they can provide a better working environment at the time of the transaction and project. Further, it is the company's responsibility to monitor their supply chain management. This means that organisations should be aware of any human rights issues in every aspect of their business including contractors and suppliers. All business operations, including those with contractors and suppliers, should follow the legal principles of the country. If the organisation finds that the national law does not actively promote international standards on human rights, the company should strive to follow the international law. There should be a compromise since the national law cannot be violated.

(ii) **Complicity and Labour Code:** Companies and organisations dealing with contractors and suppliers are also responsible for preventing and addressing complicity among employees. Complicity takes place when the organisation becomes aware of human rights abuses and provides an environment where such abuse is supported or encouraged. In terms of labour code, companies are socially responsible for avoiding compulsory and child labour. Further, there shouldn't be discrimination of labour, regardless of the project.

(iii) **Anti-corruption:** It is in the best interest of the suppliers, contractors and even the company itself if the organisation refrains from conducting or encouraging illegal methods of businesses such as corruption. Acts of corruption and under the table dealings not only pose risks to the company but also to the suppliers and contractors. Companies are responsible for advocating clean business practices including fair trade and proper business transactions.

5. **Responsibility towards Customers:** A business cannot work without customers. The survival and growth of a business depends on customer satisfaction, service and support. The commercial organisation should win the confidence of the customers. This is possible by following a positive attitude towards customers and fulfilling following social responsibilities towards them:

(i) **Quality:** The company should produce quality goods. The company should try to improve its quality because at no time can quality be 100%. There is always room for improvement of quality.

(ii) **Fair Prices:** The customers should not be cheated by charging high prices. It is not possible to fool the customer at all times. Thus, fair prices convert a customer into a permanent customer.

(iii) **Honest Advertising:** The customers want to know the facts, features, advantages, side-effects, etc, of the product. The advertisement conveys this information. Thus, the company must see that the advertisement is not being misleading and it must be done by providing the true and actual information.

(iv) **After Sales Service:** The company is expected to provide after sales service for maintenance of goods during the period of warranty. Efficient and effective after sales service helps to establish good relations between the customers and the company.

(v) **Research and Development:** The consumers require that the business organisation must conduct research and development for the purpose of improving quality and reducing cost of production. That is, it must provide ISI or AGMARK products to the customers.

(vi) **Consumer's Safety:** The business must ensure that the product supplied will not adversely affect the life and health of the customers. Unsafe products must not be marketed by the company.

(vii) **Regular Supply:** Consumers should be supplied with the goods regularly as and when required by them. Commercial organisations should not create artificial shortage of goods.

(viii) **Attend Complaints:** Consumer complaints must be attended immediately.

(ix) **Avoid Monopolistic Competition:** Commercial organisations should avoid monopolistic competition in the interest of consumers.

(x) **Training:** Commercial organisations should arrange to train customers either free or for a fee. It must be in case of computers, etc.

6. **Responsibility towards Competitors:** Competitors are other businessmen or organisations involved in a similar type of business. The existence of competition helps the business to become more dynamic and innovative so as to make itself better than its competitors. It also sometimes encourages the business to indulge in negative activities such as, resorting to unfair trade practices. The responsibilities of a business towards its competitors are:

   (i) Not to offer exceptionally high sales commission to distributors, agents etc.;

   (ii) Not to offer to customers heavy discounts and /or free products in every sale; and

   (iii) Not to defame competitors through false or ambiguous advertisements.

7. **Responsibility towards Government:** Business activities are governed by rules and regulations framed by the government. Various responsibilities of a business towards government are:

(i) **Observation of Rules and Regulation:** Organisations are required to follow the rules and regulations laid by the government in a proper manner.

(ii) **Payment of Taxes:** Business organisations must pay taxes and duties regularly to the government such as sales tax, income tax, octroi duty, custom duty, VAT, etc. Non payment of taxes is an offense, because it would be difficult for the government to undertake development programmes.

(iii) **Assistance in Implementing Socio-Economic Policies:** The government expects co-operation and help from the business sector to help in implementing programmes and policies relating to social and economic development.

(iv) **Earning Foreign Exchange:** The government also expects business organisations to earn foreign currency by exporting goods in the foreign market. The government requires this foreign currency for importing valuable and important products.

(v) **Advising the Government:** Business organisation have to provide timely advice to the government in respect of framing important policies such as Industrial policy, Import and Export policy, Licensing policy, etc.

(vi) **No Favours:** Commercial organisations should not take any type of favour from government officials by bribing or influencing them.

(vii) **Contributing to Government Treasury:** Commercial organisation must contribute funds to the government during emergencies and natural calamities such as floods, earthquakes, etc.

(viii) **Political Stability:** Commercial organisations should work towards the political stability of the country. A stable government often brings more returns and peace in a democratic country.

8. **Responsibility towards Society:** A society consists of individuals, groups, organisations, families etc. They are all collectively members of society. They interact with each other and are also dependent on each other in almost all activities. There exists a relationship among them, which may be direct or indirect. Business, being a part of society, also maintains its relationship with all other members of society. Thus, it has certain responsibilities towards society, which may be as follows:

(i) **Protection of Environment:** Pollution is a major problem of the present times, which is due to commercial organisations. Air pollution and water pollution are due to industries, chemical plants, cement plants, etc. Business organisations should take all possible measures to minimise pollution.

(ii) **Reasonable use of Resources:** Business organisation should make proper use of available resources in the large interest of the society. Resources such as fuel, water, land, etc. must be used economically.

(iii) **Reservation for Weaker Sections:** Commercial organisations are expected to provide jobs and employment opportunities for lifting up economically weaker sections of the society.

(iv) **No Participation in Anti-Social Activities:** Organisations should not participate in such activities which will adversely affect society in general. No financial help should be provided to such anti-social activities.

(v) **Development of Backward Regions:** The society requires that a business organisation should be started in backward areas. This will create employment opportunities and increase purchasing power among the rural population of India.

(vi) **Financial Assistance:** The society expects donations and financial assistance for various social causes, such as eradication of poverty, illiteracy, etc. They expect organisations to take part in anti-drug campaigns, anti-noise campaigns, and so on.

(vii) **Prevent Congestion in Cities:** Companies should also work to avoid congestion in cities spreading their industries in different places or locations.

(viii) **Employment Generation:** Business firms should make all possible efforts to generate employment. Such effort will help to solve problems caused due to unemployment in the society.

It is better to be proactive towards a problem rather than be reactive to it. One part of Social Responsibility is being responsible to people, for the actions of people that affect people. Hence, it means obligation of a business towards different social group, i.e., the consumers, employees, shareholders, society, government, media, and so on. As Abraham Lincoln once said "public sentiments is everything". With public sentiments nothing can fail, without it, nothing can succeed.

*"It is the duty of a business to provide fair returns to the shareholders, fair working conditions to the employees, fair deal to the suppliers and customers to make the business an asset to the local community and the nation."* **Earnest Dale**

### 4.2.3 Relationship between Corporate Social Responsibility and Business Ethics

Every business operates within a society. It uses the resources of the society and depends on the society for its functioning. This creates an obligation on the part of business to look after the welfare of society. So all the activities of a business should be such that they will not harm rather they will protect and contribute to the interests of the society.

Corporate social responsibility refers to all such duties and obligations of business directed towards the welfare of society. These duties can be a part of the routine functions of carrying on business activity or they may be an additional function of carrying out welfare activity.

Business ethics and corporate social responsibility are therefore two concepts many feel go hand in hand for organisations in the business environment. Business ethics are the moral values and principles a company uses to ensure all employees act in an acceptable way when involved in any business activity.

Corporate social responsibility is usually an assumption held by governments and the general public, that businesses should not conduct themselves in a manner contradictory to cultural or societal norms.

"**Business ethics**" and "**corporate social responsibility**" are two terms that are often used interchangeably, but at the same time represent somewhat different types of business practice. Ethics, of course, is always concerned with norms and values, and is basically about what is right and wrong.

CSR on the other hand may be about these things, but doesn't have to be - lots of people take a purely economic or strategic approach to CSR without any real consideration of the normative dimensions. CSR is also, as might be expected, a lot more business-friendly than business ethics. In fact, people often tend to use CSR when they're talking about the good things companies are doing, and business ethics (or a lack of them) when talking about the bad things they do.

The term business ethics represents a combination of two very familiar words, namely "business" and "ethics". The word business is usually used to mean "any organisation whose objective is to provide goods or services for profit", whereas organisations are defined as,

(1) social entities that

(2) are goal oriented,

(3) are designed as deliberately structured and coordinated activity systems and

(4) are linked to the external environment".

One of the most important organisational elements highlighted by this definition is that organisations are indeed open systems, i.e. they must interact with the environment in order to survive. "The organisation has to find and obtain needed resources, interpret and act on environmental changes, dispose of outputs, and control and coordinate internal activities in the face of environmental disturbances and uncertainty".

The fact that business organisations are open systems means that although businesses must make a profit in order to survive they must balance their desire for profit against the needs and desires of the society within which they operate. Hence, despite the fact that in market economies business organisations are traditionally allowed some degree of discretion being "ostensibly free to choose what goods and services they produce, the markets they aim to serve and the processes by which they produce", organised societies around the world did indeed establish principles and developed rules or standards of conduct - both legal and implicit - in order to guide businesses in their efforts to earn profits in ways that do not harm society as a whole.

A firm that adopts the social response approach generally meets its legal and ethical requirements and sometimes voluntarily even goes beyond these requirements in selected cases. Finally, the highest degree of social responsibility that a firm can exhibit is the social contribution approach. Firms adopting this approach view themselves as citizens of a society and, as a result, proactively seek opportunities to contribute.

### 4.2.4 Arguments for Corporate Social Responsibility

The major arguments for the assumption of social responsibilities by business are:

1. **Public Expectations:** Social expectations of business have increased dramatically since the 1960s. Public opinion in support of business pursuing social as well as economic goals is now well solidified.

2. **Long Run Profits:** Socially responsible businesses tend to have more and secure long run profits. This is the normal result of the better community relations and improved business image that responsible.

3. **Ethical Obligation:** A business firm can and should have a conscience. Business should be socially responsible because responsible actions are right for their own sake.

4. **Public Image:** Firms seek to enhance their public image to gain more customers, better employees, access to money markets, and other benefits. Since the public considers social goals to be important, business can create a favourable public image by pursuing social goals.

5. **Better Environment:** Involvement by business can solve difficult social problems, thus creating a better quality of life and a more desirable community in which to attract and hold skilled employees.

6. **Discouragement of Further Government Regulation:** Government regulation adds economic costs and restricts management's decision flexibility by becoming socially responsible, business can expect less government regulation.

7. **Balance of Responsibility and Power:** Business has a large amount of power in society. An equally large amount of responsibility is required to balance it. When power is significantly greater than responsibility, the imbalance encourages irresponsible behaviour that works against the public good.

8. **Stockholder Interests:** Social responsibility will improve the price of a business's stock in the long run. The stock market will view the socially responsible company as less risky and open to public attack. Therefore, it will award its stock a higher price earning ratio.

9. **Possession of Resources:** Business has the financial resources, technical experts, and managerial talent to provide support to public and charitable projects that need assistance.

10. **Superiority of Prevention over Cures:** Social problems must be dealt with at sometime. Business should act on them before they become serious and costly to correct and take management's energy away from accomplishing its goal of production goods and services.

## 4.2.5 Arguments against Corporate Social Responsibility

The major arguments against the assumption of social responsibilities by business are:

1. **Violation of Profit Maximisation:** This is the essence of the classical viewpoint. Business is most socially responsible when it attends strictly to its economic interests and leaves other activities to other institutions.

2. **Dilution of Purpose:** The pursuit of social goals dilutes business's primary purpose: economic productivity. Society may suffer as both economic and social goals are poorly accomplished.

3. **Costs:** Many socially responsible activities do not pay their own way. Someone has to pay these costs. Business must absorb these costs or pass them on to consumers in higher prices.

4. **Too Much Power:** Business is already one of the most powerful institutions in our society. If it pursued social goals, it would have even more power. Society has given business enough power.

5. **Lack of Skills:** The outlook and abilities of business leaders are oriented primarily toward economies. Business people are poorly qualified to cope with social issues.

6. **Lack of Accountability:** Political representatives pursue social goals and ar6e held accountable for their actions. Such is not the case with business leaders. There are no direct lines of social accountability from the business sector to the public.

7. **Lack of Broad Public Support:** There is no broad mandate from society for business to become involved in social issues. The public is divided on the issue. In fact, it is a topic that usually generates a heated debate. Actions taken under such divided support are likely to fail.

## 4.3 Justice and Economic System Ethics

The judiciary or the justice system according to Gautam Pherwani in his book "Business Ethics" is the third political institution in addition to the legislature and executive or government.

Is law a source of ethical standards, and what is the relationship between law and ethics? It is important to understand that ethics and law are distinct categories. By law or the justice system, we generally mean legislation, statutes, and regulations made by the government on a host of subjects for the public good and public welfare. Laws do not, and are not intended to, incorporate ethical principles or values, but sometimes ethical standards will be reflected in laws. For example, both morality and the law prohibit the act of murdering another human being. Similarly, legislation regulating the legal profession or other professions may give legal effect to certain professional codes of conduct. It is possible to argue, therefore, that codes of conduct regulating legal practice have the force of law. However, on a whole range of subjects from business practice to driving a vehicle, laws do not set ethical standards.

It is important to appreciate, therefore, that ethical standards are not necessarily written down in the form of laws or other rules, but represent the collective experience of a society as it regulates the behaviour of those who make up that society. The fact that an ethical standard is not repeated or copied in a law does not affect the validity of that ethical standard. However, where ethical standards are incorporated into law, such as, the right to choose an abortion, although people must obey the law, they are not necessarily required to hold the same ethical beliefs expounded by that law.

Sometimes, laws can conflict with ethical standards. For example, laws promoting apartheid in South Africa and slavery in the United States were both clearly in violation of ethical standards relating to the dignity of the person, but were nevertheless lawful and were expected to be obeyed when in force. From time to time, a mass movement develops against a particular law or set of laws, reflecting a section of public opinion that claims that the law is wrong and should therefore be repealed.

Where there is a deliberate disregard of the law by those protesting its wrongness, the result can be acts of civil disobedience. For example, in India, during the British colonial period, Mahatma Gandhi advocated and practiced civil disobedience to British laws because he and his followers wanted an end to the colonisation of their country. Similarly, in the United States, activists in the civil rights movement deliberately flouted laws that were racially discriminatory, and civil rights workers were prepared to be arrested and jailed in pursuit of equal treatment for all citizens.

Businesses are the most significant institution in the economic structure. As such, businesses are expected to produce goods and services that are demanded by members of society, and once produced, these goods and services must be distributed to the numerous societal groups. Decisions are made within the business structure about who will produce, how much will be produced, how production will be implemented, how the work will be organised, and how the finished good or service will be made available to the consuming members of society. All these decisions are necessary in the day-to-day operation of an economic institution, and all these choices are made by people. It could be argued that computer models are used to make decisions, but it can be further counter-argued that computer models are developed by people and they are the ones who implement recommendations made by computer modelling.

In order for people in all institutions to make choices, there must be some guidelines or principles upon which the choices are based. These guidelines are often referred to as values. Everyone develops a set of values, or preferences, be ginning in early childhood or perhaps even immediately from birth. These values stem from how people are raised, where they live, their ancestry, and all the other factors that influence everyone's lives. If everyone has a value system, everyone must have an ethical system upon which to base judgments and choices. Stemming from this personal set of values will come policies and procedures that will guide all organisations within the economic structure.

Boulding (1968) argued that individuals have a 'real' personal ethic, which can be deduced from a person's actual behavior, and a 'verbal' ethic, which can be deduced from a person's statements. Boulding found that it is basically a universal phenomenon that a person will talk about one set of ethical principles but act according to another. The old statement "Do as I say, not as I do" sums up accurately the perception of reality.

Ethics, from an economist's perspective, is a matter of choice. Economics is a matter of choice. There are several alternatives from which a choice has to be made. A business owner or manager might have to decide between producing weapons for military use or firearms for use by private individuals who pursue the sport of wild game hunting. These decisions are not always easy, especially when guided by the need for the organisation to make a profit. The choice that is ultimately made is based on a value system that influences policies and procedures in a given organisation. In an economic environment, the decision is often made based on values that have been determined to be most important or that are ranked on a scale of best to worst.

A dilemma that faces all decision-makers, especially, when group decision making is used, is the different value systems that are held by individuals. While organisations have policies and procedures, not every option from which to choose is necessarily easily defined or clearly understood. Many organisations have mechanisms through which those affected by the decision can go in for appeal for further consideration. In the case of a university student who receives a failing grade but thinks the grade was undeserved because of a conflict with the professor, an appeal by the student might be heard and a decision could be made to overturn the professor's decision. Or, the decision might be made in favour of the professor and the student's appeal denied. Such a decision is based on value systems that guide ethical behaviours.

Decisions made by economic institutions do not always match up with what the general populace thinks is correct. When this happens, the outcome could be the enactment of new laws or rules in order to contain those are perceived as violating the public trust. For example, many laws have been passed to curb problems like pollution. Anti-pollution laws are designed to reduce the harmful effects of pollution; when a business does not follow the laws, it can be severely penalised. In some cases, the new laws force the closure of business enterprises because conformity to the laws is cost-prohibitive. This was the case when laws went into effect requiring underground gasoline tanks at service stations to meet Environmental Protection Agency requirements. Many businesses could not meet the requirements because of the expenses involved and, therefore, had to shut down.

At other times, businesses choose to violate the laws in order to save money. In the long run, this can cost more than the business would have had to pay had the changes been made to comply with the laws. This occurred when a chemical manufacturing company was caught dumping hazardous waste into a river in Illinois. The company was told to stop the dumping and was fined a large sum of money. But during the time the environmental inspectors were on the premises, the company chose to dump more waste into the river, saying that if they had not done it, there could have been a fatal accident in the plant. They were fined an additional sum. These examples illustrate choices that must be made, not by businesses in economic systems, but by individuals in the businesses.

It was stated earlier that businesses are the most significant institution within a given economic structure. It should also be noted, however, that businesses are not the only institutions within an economic structure. There are many other important groups, such as, the family, government, churches, and schools. All these institutions play an important role in developing value systems and the moral influences on individuals in businesses.

Because many other institutions influence the thinking of individuals in organisations, different value systems are developed. Some value systems are inconsistent with what is necessary for successful business operations and become a threat to a business and economic system. An example of that is honesty. An individual whose value system does not include complete honesty becomes a threat to successful business operations. Because of threats like these to economic entities, rules are established to deal with those who have different value systems. The rules are called laws, and the government is the largest enforcer of laws.

The Governments are important to successful business and economic operations. This is so, since they help to assure fair trade and commerce within a country and internationally. A good example of this is when the U.S. government ordered the break-up of the Bell Telephone System several years ago, it was felt that the system had grown too large and that fair competition was not possible. When companies become monopolies, they can set prices and control supplies of goods and services in ways that might not be fair to consumers. Therefore, governmental intervention becomes inevitable for ensuring fair trade practices. As a logical corollary to it, many laws have been enacted to influence fair economic trade.

## Setting Business Ethical Standards

Businesses make decisions that influence consumers, employees, and society, in general. It is people who make up the businesses, and it is people who must set the standards for ethical conduct. The process for setting standards needs to be a top-down approach – management must develop and support an ethical code. The employees must understand what is expected of them in order to follow the codes. The managers and employees must therefore be trained to interpret and consider alternatives relative to established ethical codes. In larger businesses, compliance offices are often established to ensure that ethical codes are followed.

People outside the business must also know what ethical standards are being followed, and they must know that individuals within the company who do not follow the prescribed ethical codes will be dealt with in a manner appropriate to the violation. This illustrates the need to enforce the ethical codes. If a business establishes an ethical code but does not enforce it, the code will not be followed.

## 4.4 Business Ethics and Environment Protection:
### Ethics Relating to Environment Protection

The earth's resources are finite and limited. The growth of human civilisation has run parallel with increased consumption of material goods and the consequent irreversible exploitation of natural resources. Environmental changes that have occurred owing to rapid industrialisation and global trade have posed serious problems of ecological imbalances and environmental degradation.

The role of business and industry in such degradation of environment raises moral problems requiring moral solutions. Pollution, for ethical analysis, means man's adverse intervention in nature. Not only environmentalists but even businessmen have to ask themselves such moral questions and decide the extent of trade-offs between environmental damage and production of material goods. Clean air, unpolluted water, fertile land teeming with life and salubrious surroundings are desired by every man. But, so does every man aspire for a large house, with all kinds of electrical and electronic gadgets to play with, and big and varied automobiles to move around. There must be a trade-off between what all the present and future inhabitants of the earth need and what only a fortunate few can obtain and enjoy.

A brief survey of major polluting agencies and their pollutants discharged into air, water and earth gives an idea of the problem. The solutions are many and varied : finding alternatives to harmful products, especially herbicides and pesticides, implementation of safety procedures during manufacture, storage, transportation and actual use at the user-end, proper mining and quarrying practices without wounding the earth, afforestation practices to become an integral part of the timber industry, intelligent and long-term directed waste disposal strategies, and so on. The question of nuclear energy, prevention of radiation hazards and waste disposal call for a concerted co-operative endeavour from all mankind. Automobiles which have given mobility to our human race are yet another issue to be judged and evaluated as an environmental factor depending on the stage of economic growth. Environmental issues thus call for wisdom, vision, ingenuity and ethical activism on the part of the modern man.

Man has taken the bounties of nature like air, water and earth for granted, for far too long. He has built factories which gobble up non-renewable resources like arable land, oil, metals and minerals. Not only that, he lets out toxic wastes into the air, rivers and streams and thus pollutes them. Forests are denuded and the loose soil laid bare for the sun and the wind to scour it away. Strip mining is still practised and this leaves the land looking pockmarked and diseased. The degradation of the environment which had been insidious and gradual, has now assumed alarming proportions. An increasing number of species of plants and animals are being rendered extinct and their collective loss is inestimable. The role of business and industry in the degradation of our environment brings forth many important moral problems and calls for moral solutions.

It is noteworthy that concern for the human and natural environment has been growing since the end of the Second World War. People became aware of damage to wildlife and their habitat, resulting from human activities. Pollution, deforestation, and the burning of fossil fuels were discovered to be the agents of previously unsuspected and unexplained phenomenon, such as acid rain, ozone depletion and global warming. It has now dawned on thinking men that the earth's resources are finite. The environmental damage cannot be halted without movement away from the present unfocused and morally incoherent policies aimed at continual economic growth. This is a result of realising the simple truth that man's intervention in the environment has been disastrous and led to rather irreversible damage and complications as of now has not yet been fully realised.

Agriculture may be deemed to be man's first challenge to nature, and, incidentally, his first defeat. Over-grazing and over-cropping were the first of his excesses which led to the loss of fertility of the soil. Ancient Sumeria (modern Iraq) turned into a desert owing to man's folly. Soil erosion and increasing salinity by the depletion of ground water sources complicated the problem further. This is not to say that he has not learned any lesson. He goes about consuming other natural resources like minerals, coal and oil, with gay abandon like the biblical prodigal son. In fact, as pillagers and predators, we surpass all other species under the sun. It was our lopsided thinking that made us claim 'conquest of nature' as our goal. Now, we are not so certain who has conquered whom. This has been the tragedy of the present ecological crisis.

### 4.4.1 Concern for Future Generation

What factors force man to persist in taking this risk to his very survival? Growth in civilisation and expanding demand for material goods underlie his efforts. A rising population puts increasing pressure on natural resources. Industrial progress must keep pace with the demand for a decent standard of living for billions of people on earth. Added to this, is the undercurrent of concern for future generations, say 'the grandchildren of our grandchildren' as Diana Wales so succinctly and hopefully expressed it.

(1) The environment might be regarded as a proxy for the best interests of future generations and it is these stakeholders with whom the business is really interacting when it impacts on the environment. A business that has long-term aspirations needs to be aware of its impacts on future generations. It needs to conduct itself in such a way that is not only regarded as generally ethical by today's standards of awareness and understanding, but by the standards that will be applied by future generations.

(2) Each generation in every nation has an inherent right to its fair share of nature's bounties, such as air, water and land, for sustaining and enjoying life on earth in a meaningful and fruitful manner.

## 4.4.2 Polluting Activities

Pollution of the environment is, in one sense, a commonly occurring phenomenon. When it occurs in nature owing to bio-geological changes, such as, volcanic eruptions or earthquakes or cyclonic storms, and so on, it is capable of injecting into the atmosphere many pollutants in considerable quantities to harm, if not destroy, all life coming within its range. Man has no role to play in such occurrences, although he is affected by the adverse changes. On the other hand, it is the polluting activities and acts of man, inadvertently though it might be, that pose a moral problem and challenge his ethical values, and sense of right and wrong.

We can conclude from this that 'pollution' may be described as the contamination of our living environment, i.e., air, water and earth, (the three basic elements - according to the ancients - that are the building materials of the world) with man's introduction of substances (in solid, liquid and gaseous forms, as well as nuclear radiations and noise) that cause harm to human beings and their interests. The presence of man-made toxic substances in the environment makes this world less safe and less livable. This definition accommodates pollution inside the workplace as well as outside it. Moreover, by emphasising human intervention, it brings to the fore the need to judge it as moral or immoral.

It is seen that the presence of some substances in small quantities, such as, emission from a single automobile or a small workshop or factory, is not harmful. But in large quantities, it will definitely cause considerable harm. However, there are certain substances which cause great harm even in small quantities. Hence, 'pollution' is relative to the potential for harm that the substance can cause. Thus, prevention of harm by pollutants means analysing the degree of harm, its nature, and the means which can be adopted to prevent it. This calls for a thorough ethical consideration of the production of the substance until its final safe disposal.

## 4.4.3 Human Interest and Eco-System

Environmentalists are not the only ones who may oppose economic activities like, mining, timber-cutting, and manufacturing, in the name of conservation of nature including wildlife. Even businessmen have to ask themselves such moral questions as are posed before them, in the long-term interest of their business. As, for instance, they might ask whether it would matter if their action caused a species to become extinct; if it caused death of individual animals; and whether it caused widespread erosion, at some distance of time or farther away from their seat of action. Is the extinction of a species, or pristine natural scenery, an acceptable price to pay for increased employment opportunities? To put it bluntly, how to determine the complex trade-offs between growth, lifestyles and protecting and preserving the environment?

In order to weigh the eco-systems against human and other interests, it is necessary to presume that we accept eco-systems as normally considerable, and that **the modification of eco-systems are often contrary to long-term human interests**. There, certainly, arise cases of genuine conflicts where the different moral considerations pull in different directions. In evaluating our moral concerns, we have to ask ourselves many basic questions:

1. Is there pollution? Is it recognisable clearly as such?
2. What kind of pollution is caused? What degree of pollution is caused?
3. How is it caused? At what stage or stages? What factors cause it?
4. Is the quantum of pollution relatively or absolutely dangerous?
5. Who are the carriers? What is the mode of transmission of pollutants?
6. Can a 'Paper Trace' be made from the stage of procuring the raw materials to the stages of (a) sale and consumption of the finished product? and (b) collection and neutralisation or denaturing of wastes upto their final and safe disposal ?
7. Is it possible and practical to prevent or check or reduce or control the production of wastes and/or the adverse effect on the eco-system harming humans and other living beings within reasonable costs? Is society capable of paying for it? In other words, what is the trade-off against what?

This brings us to the first stage of our analysis of environmental ethics.

Further, many other complex questions may arise. Who should decide how clean and healthful air and water should be? Who are the stakeholders involved? Who are affected to what extent and who should compensate them, and what is the nature of compensation that might satisfy the affected? The problem becomes more intricate if the nature of harm (such as, death, bodily harm or suffering or genetic disorders) cannot truly be compensated in the proper sense. Therefore, in the second stage of our analysis, we have to ask these further questions:

(i) Is there any alternative available? Is it available immediately? Or, is there possibility of an alternative being (made) available (by scientific research or technological innovation) in a short while? What is the time lag involved? Can the present activities be suspended or held up until a new alternative is found and employed?

(ii) Who should take the above decision? - Producer or Producers' Forum or Government or Governments and affected countries on behalf of the public?

(iii) What kind of responsibility devolves and on whom - such as, legal, corporate, social or ethical?

(iv) What kind of moral audit is feasible and done and by whom?

### 4.4.4 Environmental Ethics

Generally speaking, we must carefully consider the different moral issues, weigh how important they are, and arrive at a sound judgement. It may be useful to remind ourselves of an obvious truth about environmental ethics. "There is no decisive calculus available to assist us in these judgements. It is not correct to say that humans should always come first nor is it correct to say that preserving an eco-system is always more important than protecting any set of human interests."

There is, however, yet another aspect of the problem. Clean air, unpolluted water and salubrious surroundings are desired by all. At the same time, most people desire materialistic prosperity in the form of white goods, T. V. sets, computers, motor cars, large houses, and so on. Is it possible to have the goods and not pay the hidden costs? Here, it is apt to use the often repeated cliché that there is no such thing called a free lunch. But, is it not unfair to expect an innocent bystander to pay for one's lunch? For, it is exactly what happens when the producer creates wastes and allows them to pollute the environment without proper disposal. The external costs which are borne ultimately by the public are both unjust and immoral.

### 4.4.5 Survey of Polluting Practices

A brief survey of the major polluting industries and practices may be in order so that we can understand the behavioural patterns of businessmen. Foreign intrusions into the environment will include smoke and emissions from manufacturing industries, chemical and metal processing industries, oil refineries, as major sources, where fossil fuels like, coal and oil are burnt. Automobiles and trucks are mobile sources of polluting gases. Cigarette smoke is just as harmful both to the smokers and non-smokers exposed to passive smoking. That apart, products like, plastic, steel, aluminium and electricity cannot be produced or generated without toxic by-products.

The manufacture of known toxic substances like, pesticides and herbicides, and intermediate chemicals and products for the manufacture of fertilisers and plastics, vinyl chlorides, synthetic rubber, asbestos and its products, must be undertaken with a full awareness of its dangers and risks, to the workers as well as the ultimate handlers. The importance of maintaining a very high safety standard irrespective of the work culture of the place where the plant is located, and scrupulous insistence on technologically rigorous design and maintenance of the chemical plant are the key factors brought out by the avoidable tragedy at Bhopal. An accident that occurred in the Union Carbide plant in Bhopal caused the death of 2,500 people; with partial or permanent injury and disability to over 86,000 persons. This was the worst case of industrial pollution in the world.

The development of modern chemistry and its corollary increasing industrialisation have adversely affected our scarce water resources. Effluents from such industries are known to contain assimilable nitrogen and phosphates, which when discharged into rivers and streams promote the over-growth of algae to the detriment of fish and other organisms, ultimately leading to the extinction of all life. The constant attempts to clean the European rivers and waterways, the clamour for cleaning up the much abused Mediterranean Sea, and the Ganga river nearer home, are many glaring illustrations of water pollution. It is observed that Lake Erie has become overwhelmed by pollutants and has 'in effect died'. Sewage and industrial wastes and the run-offs from heavily fertilised farmlands have 'loaded the lake waters with excess of phosphates and nitrates as to jar on the biology of the lake permanently out of balance. Result: 'the fish have all but gone'.

It is quite true that the use of fertilisers and pesticides and herbicides has been a boon to farmers and yielded increased crops to feed the burgeoning populations of the world. At the same time, the side effect has been deleterious as the excess has seeped into the ground and polluted the ground water and wells. The excess has run off into rivers and streams, killing fish and contaminating them. Consumption of the fish catch from these polluted waters has caused the toxic substances to enter the food chain of humans, thus completing a vicious circle. Cancer, birth deformities and many other ills have resulted from this. In the beginning, the nature of harm done was not clearly known, and it was unintentional; but now that the link has been clearly established. Therefore, the question arises as to whether is it not possible to develop pesticides and herbicides which will not eventually and indirectly harm men and their interests? The promotion of less harmful and harmless alternatives must be encouraged and, government initiative and control will become necessary to implement the alternatives. It is unreasonable to accept greater risks and the present actual harms caused by the chemical products known to be harmful and outlawed for that reason, in the countries of their origin.

Soil pollution is yet another facet of this problem. As already pointed out, unscientific use of pesticides and herbicides to control pests, and the over-use of fertilisers, make the land contaminated in the long run. Further, they seep into the soil, and change the land quality. Mining, quarrying and foresting activities spoil the land value and make it unfit for future. The serious nature of despoliation caused by the timber trade may be gauged from this quotation: "Few industries can rival the short-termism of the timber trade," concluded a recent report from the Environmental Investigation Agency (EIA). Arguing that the $100 billion (₹ 390,000 crores) world timber industry was 'running out of control,' the EIA noted that the unbridled plunder of the planet's remaining rain forests is increasing at an alarming rate."

Disposal of toxic and non-bio-degradable wastes has added yet another important ethical dimension to the problem. Petrochemicals and plastics, as well as the by-products and wastes generated during their production, have been found to be highly toxic and often carcinogenic and non-biodegradable. They will continue to haunt the coming generations with disease, suffering and death. In the beginning, toxic wastes were buried underground, or thrown into rivers and streams, or just abandoned on waste land, without a thought, and without any safeguards. The penalty that an innocent third party, i.e., the general public has to pay for this unethical action has never been brought out more forcefully than in the cases of the Love Canal and the Times Beach waste disposal case.

### 4.4.6 Ethical Responsibility

The manufacturers have an ethical responsibility to oversee the safe use and disposal of their wastes belonging to producers. Just because they do not want their wastes, it does not release them from their responsibility for them, until they dispose off their wastes safely and finally without causing harm to others. The damage to environment impinges on other's rights to life, health, freedom, and dignity.

As an absolute ban on pollution is unrealistic and impractical, and the cost of eliminating all pollution would be forbiddingly excessive, it will then be necessary to determine the extent of pollution that is acceptable. Once determined, a strong social momentum should be forthcoming to enforce the regulations effectively to halt the environmental damage. In economic costs, the external costs to society are not borne by the polluters. The producer dumps the wastes in the earth (belonging to all) and escapes scot free - at best with nothing or at worst at a very lower rates, and the innocent third parties (like, the general public) are made to pay for in terms of poor health and reduced longevity.

The greatest single source of contamination of the whole planet is radioactivity. It is needless to belabour the point that nuclear tests cause fallouts which contaminate every part of the earth's surface and all its inhabitants, and all flora and fauna. All radioactive materials are, without exception, are unanimously recognised as most highly toxic with their effect lasting upto 250,000 years or even more. They cause deadly diseases like, cancer, and cause mutation of cells and genes, leading to sterility, birth of deformed babies, or congenital disorders, great suffering and premature ageing. The ethical problem that is posed is precisely related to the need for nuclear power in the face of such findings.

Fossil fuel burning and automobile exhausts pour into the atmosphere sulphur and nitrogen-related oxides which in contact with the atmosphere turn into sulphuric acid and nitric acid. They come back to haunt the earth in the form of rain and snow. This acid rain destroys life in forests, lakes and soil, by upsetting the delicate balance in nature. Acid rain is a short term result of burning fossil fuels. Its long-term effect is even more insidious. The increased amount of carbon dioxide poured into the atmosphere creates a shield around the earth, which does not permit heat to radiate out of the earth. Thereby, global temperatures go up, leading to a 'Greenhouse Effect'. Further, the rise in temperature will cause the sea levels to rise, submerging coastal and low-lying lands. Possibly, temperate zones will become deserts.

Nuclear power looks safer as it does not generate acid rains or the 'Greenhouse Effect'. It was considered to be a clean, efficient and low-cost producer of electricity. However, in course of time, its disadvantages and drawbacks came to the fore with devastating effect.

There exists the risk of cancer and other deadly disorders to minors working in uranium mines, and those who handle it. Continued radioactivity of mine tailings has been noted. Safety precaution of the highest order is called for, for all the persons working in the facilities as well as for the residents nearby. Even so, people living near the plant are put to great risk of a nuclear accident or meltdown. It may be a kind of compensation for them that they are able to get jobs and good payment.

On the other hand, the majority of the people living far away from the nuclear plant and, therefore, not courting any risk, are the ones who derive the benefits of electric power. The amount of risk that people wish to take in exchange for benefits received is not merely an ethical question. It is also a social issue to be settled by a political process with a built-in factor of people's rights.

### 4.4.7 Disposal of Waste

Finally, the question of disposal of nuclear waste as well as electronic waste from abandoned computers, TVs, mobiles, etc., has still been unresolved and hangs like an albatross round the necks of nuclear nations. The toxic wastes are radioactive almost permanently (lasting upto 250,000 years or more). Till date, no methods have been devised to prevent the release of radioactive materials into ground water. The sealed steel containers containing the toxic wastes will get rusted and corroded at intervals, and the contents have got to be repacked and released and stored several times in the course of their existence at enormous costs and untold risks. The cost of guarding the nuclear waste to prevent its falling into the hands of terrorists and undesirable maniacs will be prohibitive and may prove to be burdensome for the future generations. No one will be ready to accept the waste disposed off in his area. Is it just to ask the future generations to deal with the toxic garbage including nuclear waste that we have produced?

The world needs electricity. It is more so for the poor countries of the Third World. It is morally incumbent upon the developed nations like, the USA and Western Europe to be prudent and conservative in the use of electricity and thus save enormous quantities of oil and coal. Alternative and cleaner sources of electricity, such as, the solar and geo-thermal sources, have got to be harnessed with greater application. The need of the hour is to develop better solar batteries and cells. Here is a technical challenge of rare humanism and ethical business opportunity of a lifetime.

### 4.4.8 Socio-Political Dimension of Pollution Control

Pollution can be controlled and handled. Hence, it acquires a socio-political dimension. The problem of deciding all the facets and dimensions of pollution are sometimes complex, but nevertheless, it is capable of analysis. Those who produce the wastes are morally obliged to dispose off them in safe ways. Otherwise, they are morally guilty of doing harm to others. Hence, the law was made requiring a 'paper trace' of handling such wastes from the producing plant through proper and final disposition in a proper facility.

The moral attitude towards the unintended victims of pollution would be to compensate them for the harm done to them. This is a form of licensing. Airport facilities may compensate the affected neighbours by buying up their property in a generous way. The second approach is for the firm to eliminate or clean up pollution before it damages anyone. A third view would be for the firm to prevent pollution at the source. The government may mandate the nature of pollution or effluents to be prevented, leaving the actual technological method or measures to be employed to the best abilities of the firm concerned. This will give proper incentive to the firm to find cost-effective means of preventing pollution.

Alternatives for pollution control include:

1. **Role of the Individual**

The responsibility for reducing pollution falls equally on individuals as on communities and organisations. The car user should use lead-free petrol for the catalytic converters to reduce pollution. Otherwise, he is guilty of harming others. The manufacturers are liable to pass on the additional cost of pollution control (which also includes the cost of waste disposal) to the customers. If the resulting product becomes too expensive to buy, then, people as an inherent component of a given society will have to decide whether or not they want the product more than clean air.

The problem of pollution control is thus seen to be complex and throws up several alternative solutions, each of which has to be decided with a high sense of ethical responsibility. It is, therefore, necessary to identify the issues which are ethically mandatory (Kantian approach) and those which are desirable but not mandatory. A moral audit can be made to evaluate a company's actions with respect to pollution.

## 2. Corporates' Responsibility

The most notable development in corporate accountability focuses particularly on their interaction with the environment and with the communities in which they operate. Nowadays, large companies religiously provide information about a wide range of information making particular reference to environmental matters, such as, waste disposal and pollution control, energy use and community involvement. This was the observation made by Alex Dunlop as late as in 1993-94. It might, perhaps, have been owing to increasing government pressure holding companies accountable for their abuse and misuse of environment earlier.

## 3. Preserving Environment - Alternatives

Many thinking persons have offered a variety of recommendations to fight pollution and for preserving the environment in order to render clean, safe, healthy and beautiful for both the present generation as well as posterity. Each of us can have a share in the responsibility according to his/her ability. For everyone can deny himself with a sense of pride and sacrifice and show self-restraint.

'Simple living and high thinking' is a very sensible and practical motto. We can lessen our dependence on material goods without loss of happiness. Let us be conservative in the use of electricity, heat, wood, metals and plastics, water, oil and other resources. We should recycle cans, bottles, paper and other recyclable things. Use of fuel efficient automobiles, using lead-free petrol, and proper maintenance of vehicles to give maximum efficiency, are prudent acts. Use of solar power is high priority. Reforestation, tree planting in waste lands must become national practice.

## 4.5 Business Ethics and Consumer Protection

A product is the most important link between the producer and the consumer. The consumer looks for several attributes in the product, such as, the physical ones like quality and performance, implied ones like reliability and warranty, and psychological ones like, the corporate image and the product image. Behind every attribute of the product, there occurs a host of ethical and legal issues. When producers fail to disclose the risks associated with the product by providing information about its function, nature or use, or the changes made in the product with attendant risks, ethical issues arise.

Not harming others is the central principle governing corporate obligations towards its customers and others. This implies that they have a consistent responsibility for product safety as long as there is a continuous upgradation of their product as well as in their constant upgradation of their logistics of product distribution. Further, these ethical guidelines are not obviously separate from the legal issues.

As such, changes in the law from the conventional but one-sided *Caveat Emptor* to the present day obligation of "Absolute Liability" has shown how ethical views have influenced and interacted with legal obligations of the corporates with their customers and the society at large. Product safety law is still in a state of flux and has tried to bring about equity, justice and fairness to a large section of society.

## 4.5.1 Problems Faced by Consumers

Consumers may be deceived by immoral businessmen including traders, dealers, producers and manufacturers as well as service providers in various ways:

1. **Adulteration:** Adulteration refers to adding something inferior to the product being sold. This is generally found in tea leaves, edible oil, spices, cereals, petrol, etc. Sometimes, the inferior material used with the product may be injurious to health.

2. **Sale of Spurious Products:** Instead of the real product, something of no value is sold to the customer. It is often found in the case of drugs or health care products.

3. **Use of False Weights and Measures:** Goods which are sold by weight (kg.) like vegetables, cereals, sugar, etc., those sold by measures (meter) like textile fabrics, suit pieces, are sometimes found to be less than the actual weight or length. False weights or measuring tapes having false markings are used for the purpose and buyers are cheated. Sometimes packaged goods and sealed containers (tins) contain fewer quantities, than what is stated on the label or packet.

4. **Sale of Duplicates:** Goods indication a mark of superior quality than the actual. For example, goods which are locally made are sold at a higher price as imported items expected to be of superior quality.

5. **Hoarding and Black-marketing:** When stocks of essential commodity are intentionally held back by dealers and is not made available in the open market it is known as hoarding. The purpose of hoarding is to create an artificial scarcity, to push up the prices. Black marketing is the practice of selling hoarded goods, secretly at a higher price. These practices are sometimes adopted when there is short supply of any product.

6. **Tie-in-Sales:** Buyers of durable consumer goods are sometimes required to buy some other goods as a pre-condition to sale or may be required to pay after-sales service charges for one year in advance.

7. **Misleading Advertisement:** Some advertisements falsely represent a product or service to be of superior quality, grade or standard, or falsely assert the value of a product or service.

## 4.5.2 Legal Protection to Consumers

A number of laws have been passed by the Government of India over the years to protect the interest of consumers. A brief outline of the purpose of these laws in given below:

1. **Agricultural Products (Grading and Marketing) Act, 1937:** This Act provides for grading and certifying quality standard of agricultural commodities which are allowed to be stamped with AGMARK seal of the Agricultural marketing department of the Government.

2. **Industries (Development and Regulation) Act, 1951:** This Act provides for control over production and distribution of manufactured goods. According to this Act, the Central Government may order investigation of any industry, if it is of the opinion that there has been substantial fall in the volume of production, or a marked decline in the quality of a product, or any unreasonable rise in price. After due investigation, the Government may issue directions to set things right. If the directions are not acted upon, the Government may take over the concerned undertakings.

3. **Prevention of Food Adulteration Act, 1954:** This Act provides for severe punishment for adulteration of food articles. Food inspectors are appointed and they have powers to lift samples and send them for analysis. Penalties are also provided under the act for offences committed by persons with regard to manufacture, import, storage, sale and distribution of adulterated food articles.

4. **Essential Commodities Act, 1955:** Under this Act, the Government has power to declare any commodity as essential in the public interest. Thereby the Government can control the production, supply and distribution of the trading of such commodities. It also provides for action against anti-social activities of profiteers, hoarders and black-marketers.

5. **The Standards of Weights and Measures Act, 1956:** This Act provides for the use of standard weights and standard measures of length throughout the country. 'Metre' has been specified as the primary unit for measuring length, and 'kilogram' as the primary unit for measuring weight. Before this act came into force, different system of weights and measures were used in different parts of the country like 'Pound', 'Chhatak' and 'Seer' as Weights, Yard, Inch and Foot for length, etc. These differences provided opportunities for traders to exploit the consumers.

6. **Monopolies and Restrictive Trade Practices Act, 1969:** Under the provisions of this Act, as amended in 1983 and 1984, consumers and consumer groups can exercise their right of redressal by filing complaints relating to restrictive and unfair trade practices. The Government has constituted the MRTP commission which is empowered to deal

with consumer complaints after due investigation and enquiry. The Commission has power to award compensation for any loss or injury suffered by consumers.

7. **Prevention of Black-marketing and Maintenance of Essential Supplies Act, 1980:** The primary objective of this act is to provide for detention of persons with a view to prevention of black-marketing and maintenance of supplies of commodities essential to the community. The maximum detention for persons acting in any manner against the intention of the act can be imprisonment upto 6 months.

8. **Consumer Protection Act, 1986:** This Act provides for consumer protection more comprehensively than any other law. Consumers can seek legal remedy for a wide range of unfair practices not only with respect to goods but also for deficiency in services like banking, insurance, financing, transport, telephone, supply of electricity or other energy, housing, boarding and lodging, entertainment, amusement, etc. This Act also includes provision for the establishment of consumer protection councils at the centre and the state. For the settlement of consumer disputes, the act has provided for a semi-judicial system. It consists of District Forum, State Commission and National Commission for redressal of consumer disputes. These may be regarded as consumer courts.

### 4.5.3 Business Obligation towards Consumer Protection

As regards businessmen, it is expected that producers, distributors, dealers, wholesalers as well as retailers should pay due regard to consumer rights in their own interest. They should ensure supply of quality goods and services at reasonable prices. To prevent unfair practices, associations of traders, chambers of commerce and industry, and manufacturers' associations should entertain consumer complaints against their members and take proper action against those guilty of malpractice.

1. **Environmental Protection and Product Safety:**

The corporations have an obligation to environmental protection in the manufacture of their product; just as clearly as they have an obligation to ensure product safety. This is their *prima facie* second order moral obligation or the 'moral minimum' which they must meet. Causing no or little harm to environment as well as their customers is the most basic of their obligations. However, it is equally clear that people will accept some degree of risk or harm in return for greater comfort or good. When they agree to the mining of ores and quarrying, setting up timber industry, or manufacture of fertilisers and pesticides, or the production of electricity from fossil fuels or nuclear power, they are consciously inflicting a risk to their environment.

In a like manner, the people accept risks when they drive an automobile, fly in an aeroplane, or use a chain saw or a new pharmaceutical product. In all these instances, there is implied a reasonable expectation of safety in the products they use, and the implied faith in the manufacturer's knowledge and expertise that the product is safe to handle and use. If the main question that might be asked of environmental protection is, "How much harm is safe?"; whereas the most important question that we ask on product safety is : "How much safe is safe ?"

## 2. Safety Standards

It is not reasonable to expect that all products must be made as safe as possible regardless of expense. Manufacturers must only make the product as safe as the state of the art at the point of time and development. Even so, the question persists: "How much safe is safe?" The answer is obvious (and appropriate for that point in time) : Just as much safety as is attainable and practicable. This is a technical matter and must be accessible to the manufacturers. The second question is more open-ended. "How much safety is demanded with respect to a particular product or activity?" This necessarily involves the willingness to take risks on the part of the customer, or his value comparisons. This is decided by the informed customer himself or the general public or the Government acting on their behalf.

The next step follows logically: Whether or not the product comes up to the standards set by the Government or public? From this, it follows that as knowledge and techniques advance, the level of acceptance of risk will diminish. For instance, people now-a-days accept travel by aeroplanes or motor cars, living in high-rise buildings, and so on, as a matter of course, without being self-conscious of any risk, and even then they are assured of a large margin of safety.

## 3. Manufacturers' Obligation to Inform Customers

If it is true that no product can be made absolutely safe against all circumstances and eventualities, then, the question arises as to what degree of safety (or/danger) is to be made acceptable. It is obvious who should decide rationally about the risk, the end-user. But before that, the user (the general public) must know and he has a right to know that he is being put at risk of harm. It follows logically, therefore, that the manufacturer informs consumers of:

(i) the potential risk of danger to which they are exposing themselves,
(ii) the nature and source of risk, and the condition under which the risk arises,
(iii) how great it is and how to get rid of it, prevent or overcome it, and finally,
(iv) if there is any alternative and if so, what their comparative merit lies in.

At every stage, the user has the option to use (or continue to use) the product, with intelligent care taking due precautions, or avoid or cease using it altogether, or seek the alternative, if any. It is rational to accept some risk if it is necessary to achieve a greatly desired end (like, flying in an aeroplane to be in time for a business meeting). But even then it is equally rational to minimise that risk to the extent possible.

The moral imperatives of the manufacturers are clear i.e., they should produce goods that are upto the public expectations. They are obligated to inform the public about the risks they are taking when this is not the case. Otherwise, knowingly selling goods that are less safe than the public (the ordinary buyers) expect, amounts to implicit deception, violation of an implicit agreement or contract, and hence, a brazen moral defect.

The general public is not usually knowledgeable about every modern product in use, as for example, a motor car, a TV set, a mobile phone, or the medicines prescribed for use. The manufacturer knows best the precise nature and qualities of his product. The general public is justified in taking for granted the safety and efficacy of the product, and hence, it is morally imperative for the manufacturer to inform them of the risks inherent in the product, when this is the case. The theory of *Caveat Emptor* ('buyer beware') is totally inappropriate in such cases.

## 4.6 Business Ethics and Social Justice

The judiciary or the justice system according to Gautam Pherwani in his book "Business Ethics" is the third political institution in addition to the legislature and executive or government.

Is law a source of ethical standards, and what is the relationship between law and ethics? It is important to understand that ethics and law are distinct categories. By law or the justice system, we generally mean legislation, statutes, and regulations made by the government on a host of subjects for the public good and public welfare. Laws do not, and are not intended to, incorporate ethical principles or values, but sometimes ethical standards will be reflected in laws. For example, both morality and the law prohibit the act of murdering another human being. Similarly, legislation regulating the legal profession or other professions may give legal effect to certain professional codes of conduct. It is possible to argue, therefore, that codes of conduct regulating legal practice have the force of law. However, on a whole range of subjects from business practice to driving a vehicle, laws do not set ethical standards.

It is important to appreciate, therefore, that ethical standards are not necessarily written down in the form of laws or other rules, but represent the collective experience of a society as it regulates the behaviour of those who make up that society. The fact that an ethical standard is not repeated or copied in a law does not affect the validity of that ethical standard. However, where ethical standards are incorporated into law, such as, the right to choose an abortion, although people must obey the law, they are not necessarily required to hold the same ethical beliefs expounded by that law.

Businesses are the most significant institution in the economic structure. As such, businesses are expected to produce goods and services that are demanded by members of society, and once produced, these goods and services must be distributed to the numerous societal groups. Decisions are made within the business structure about who will produce, how much will be produced, how production will be implemented, how the work will be organised, and how the finished good or service will be made available to the consuming members of society.

All these decisions are necessary in the day-to-day operation of an economic institution, and all these choices are made by people. It could be argued that computer models are used to make decisions, but it can be further counter-argued that computer models are developed by people and they are the ones who implement recommendations made by computer modelling.

In order for people in all institutions to make choices, there must be some guidelines or principles upon which the choices are based. These guidelines are often referred to as values. Everyone develops a set of values, or preferences, beginning in early childhood or perhaps even immediately from birth. These values stem from how people are raised, where they live, their ancestry, and all the other factors that influence everyone's lives. If everyone has a value system, everyone must have an ethical system upon which to base judgements and choices. Stemming from this personal set of values will come policies and procedures that will guide all organisations within the economic structure.

Ethics, from an economist's perspective, is a matter of choice. Economics is a matter of choice. There are several alternatives from which a choice has to be made. A business owner or manager might have to decide between producing weapons for military use or firearms for use by private individuals who pursue the sport of wild game hunting. These decisions are not always easy, especially when guided by the need for the organisation to make a profit. The choice that is ultimately made is based on a value system that influences policies and procedures in a given organisation. In an economic environment, the decision is often made based on values that have been determined to be most important or that are ranked on a scale of best to worst.

Decisions made by economic institutions do not always match up with what the general populace thinks is correct. When this happens, the outcome could be the enactment of new laws or rules in order to contain those are perceived as violating the public trust. For example, many laws have been passed to curb problems like pollution. Anti-pollution laws are designed to reduce the harmful effects of pollution; when a business does not follow the laws, it can be severely penalised. In some cases, the new laws force the closure of business enterprises because conformity to the laws is cost-prohibitive. This was the case when laws went into effect requiring underground gasoline tanks at service stations to meet

**Environmental Protection Agency requirements:**

Many businesses could not meet the requirements because of the expenses involved and, therefore, had to shut down.

At other times, businesses choose to violate the laws in order to save money. In the long run, this can cost more than the business would have had to pay had the changes been made to comply with the laws. This occurred when a chemical manufacturing company was caught dumping hazardous waste into a river in Illinois. The company was told to stop the dumping and was fined a large sum of money. But during the time the environmental inspectors were on the premises, the company chose to dump more waste into the river, saying that if they had not done it, there could have been a fatal accident in the plant. They were fined an additional sum. These examples illustrate choices that must be made, not by businesses in economic systems, but by individuals in the businesses.

Because many other institutions influence the thinking of individuals in organisations, different value systems are developed. Some value systems are inconsistent with what is necessary for successful business operations and become a threat to a business and economic system. An example of that is honesty. An individual whose value system does not include complete honesty becomes a threat to successful business operations. Because of threats like these to economic entities, rules are established to deal with those who have different value systems. The rules are called laws, and the government is the largest enforcer of laws.

## Setting Business Ethical Standards

Businesses make decisions that influence consumers, employees, and society, in general. It is people who make up the businesses, and it is people who must set the standards for ethical conduct. The process for setting standards needs to be a top-down approach – management must develop and support an ethical code. The employees must understand what is expected of them in order to follow the codes. The managers and employees must therefore be trained to interpret and consider alternatives relative to established ethical codes. In larger businesses, compliance offices are often established to ensure that ethical codes are followed.

People outside the business must also know what ethical standards are being followed, and they must know that individuals within the company who do not follow the prescribed ethical codes will be dealt with in a manner appropriate to the violation. This illustrates the need to enforce the ethical codes. If a business establishes an ethical code but does not enforce it, the code will not be followed.

## 4.7 Role of Social Responsibility in Indian Companies

In a global CSR study undertaken in seven countries, viz., India, South Korea, Thailand, Singapore, Malaysia, The Philippines and Indonesia by the U.K.-based International Centre for CSR in 2003, India has been ranked second in the list. This ideally shows the value that is important to customers in India. Bharat Petroleum and Maruthi Udyog have been ranked as the best companies in the country. The next comes in the list are - Tata Motors and Hero Honda, Canara Bank, Indal, Gujarat Ambuja and Wipro are involved in community development work of building roads, running schools and hospitals. ACC has been rendering social service for over five decades. They are setting up schools, health centers, agro-based industries and improving the quality of rural life. BHEL is actively involved in the welfare of the surrounding communities and is helping the organisation to earn goodwill of the local people. It is also providing drinking water facilities, construction of roads and culverts, provision of health facilities, educational facilities, and so on; while companies like, ONGC are encouraging sports by providing employment to good players on their pay rolls. Tisco, Telco and Hindalco won the award for excelling in CSR, jointly given by FICCI and Business world for the year 2003.

ONGC has also committed resources by adopting a few villages to implement President Dr. Abdul Kalam's idea of PURA (Provision of Urban Amenities in Rural Areas). NTPC has established a trust to work for the cause of the physically challenged people. Similarly, in the private sector, Infosys, Wipro and Reliance are believed to be most socially responsible corporations.

In 1999, Kofi Annan of the United Nations invited corporate leaders for a Global Compact to promote nine principles covering three areas, namely, human rights, labour rights, and sustainable development. Today, India can be legitimately proud to have had the second largest number of companies from any country subscribing to the Global Compact. Several public sector companies have also joined together to form the Global Compact Society of India.

In the last twenty years, MNCs have played a key role in defining markets and influencing the behaviour of a large number of consumers. Globalisation and liberalisation have provided a great opportunity for corporations to be globally competitive by not only expanding their production base but also their market share.

Recent years have been witness to many progressive organisations of our country playing a key social role. In some of these organisations, the approach has been to take up only business-centric activities, which are directly relevant to their business. The guiding philosophy in these organisations is that social reasonability is good only if it pays.

This approach benefits both the organisation and the stakeholder, alike. Thus, ITC has been afforesting private degraded land to augment the supply of raw material for its paper factory. Similarly, Hindustan Lever which requires good quality water for the manufacture of its food products has been improving the quality of water in many communities. Companies like, Cadburys India, Glaxo and Richardson Hindustan are helping farmers to grow crops which serve as raw materials for them. Lipton in Etha district of Uttar Pradesh has started veterinary hospitals in the region from where it buys milk. British Gas (which sells compressed natural gas to India) has recently started teaching unemployed youngsters how to become mechanics for gas-based autorickshaws in Delhi. In some other organisations, the approach has been to take up such philanthropic activities in which they can make a useful difference.

The following are some examples of the same :

**Coca – Cola:**

As one of the largest and most globally spread companies in the world, Coca–Cola took seriously its ability and responsibility to positively affect the communities in which it operated. The company's mission statement, called the Coca-Cola Promise, stated : "The Coca-Cola Company exists to benefit and refresh everyone who is touched by our business." The Company has made efforts towards good citizenship in the areas of community, by improving the quality of life in the communities in which they operate, and the environment, by addressing water, climate change and waste management initiatives. Their activities also included, The Coca–Cola Africa Foundation created to combat the spread of HIV / AIDS through partnership with governments, UNAIDS, and other NGOs, and The Coca–Cola Foundation, focused on higher education as a vehicle to build strong communities and enhance individual opportunity Coca-Cola's footprint in India was significant as well. The Company employed 7,000 citizens and believed that for every direct job, 30 – 40 more were created in the supply chain. Like its parent, Coke India's Corporate Social Responsibility (CSR) initiatives were both community and environment–focused. Priorities included education, where primary education projects had been set up to benefit children in slums and villages, water conservation, where the Company supported community–based rainwater harvesting projects to restore water levels and promote conservation education, and health.

**(a) PepsiCo**

Pepsi Cola is also into helping the rural areas in their economic development. It further offered to transfer food-processing, packaging, and water-treatment technology to India. Pepsi's bundle of benefits won four 'Ps' for entering a market, Pepsi added two additional 'Ps', namely, politics and public opinion.

Similarly, almost all MNCs like, Microsoft, McDonald, Nokia, Unilever, ITC are also adopting social responsibility of business in order to have sustainable market development and growth not only in their countries but also in the host countries.

## Points to Remember

1. **Corporate social responsibility** refers to the obligations of businessmen to pursue those policies, to make those decisions, or to follow those lines of action, which are desirable in terms of objectives and values of society.

2. Businesses are responsible towards different interest groups which includes owners, investors, employees, suppliers, customers, competitors, government and society

3. **Problems Faced by Consumers**
   - Adulteration
   - Sale of Spurious Products
   - Use of False Weights and Measures
   - Sale of Duplicates
   - Hoarding and Black-marketing
   - Tie-in-Sales
   - Misleading Advertisement

4. **Legal Protection to Consumers**
   - Agricultural Products (Grading and Marketing) Act, 1937
   - Industries (Development and Regulation) Act, 1951
   - Prevention of Food Adulteration Act, 1954
   - Essential Commodities Act, 1955
   - The Standards of Weights and Measures Act, 1956
   - Monopolies and Restrictive Trade Practices Act, 1969
   - Prevention of Black-marketing and Maintenance of Essential Supplies Act, 1980
   - Consumer Protection Act, 1986

5. **Business Obligation towards Consumer Protection**
   - Environmental Protection and Product Safety
   - Safety Standards
   - Manufacturers' Obligation to Inform Customers

## Questions for Discussion

1. Define corporate social responsibility.
2. Bring out arguments clearly for and against social responsibility.
3. What is the relationship between ethics and social justice?
4. How are ethics related to environmental protection?
5. Discuss the relationship between social responsibility and consumer protection.

# Chapter 5...

# Functional Ethics

## Contents ...
- 5.1 Introduction
- 5.2 Meaning of Functional Ethics
- 5.3 Types of Ethics According to Functions of Business/Functional Ethics
- 5.4 Copyrights, IPR, Trademarks and Business Ethics
- 5.5 Ethical Challenges for Managers in the 21st Century
- • Points to Remember
- • Questions for Discussion

## Learning Objectives ...
- ➢ To explore the meaning of functional ethics
- ➢ To analyse the different types of business ethics according to the various functions of business
- ➢ To elaborate the role of business ethics in the context of copyrights, IPR and Trademarks
- ➢ To examine the ethical challenges for managers in the 21st century

## 5.1 Introduction

Business ethics has not only been recognised as increasingly important, but has also undergone rapid changes and developments during the past decade or so. Business ethics can be said to begin where law ends.

As the field of Business Ethics is widely debated, it has been broken down into the various functional areas of business itself, so that each area and each issue can be looked at individually. By grouping business ethics along business functions, one can develop ease of understanding. Also, each individual functioning under different business areas can concentrate only on the ethics of each area, thus helping him grasp the business ethics code of his company.

## 5.2 Meaning of Functional Ethics

In a large organisation, it is usually easier to identify separate functional areas because people work together in departments. Each department carries out the tasks that relate to its particular area. The main purpose of functional areas is to ensure that all important business activities are carried out efficiently. This is essential if the business is to achieve its aims and objectives. In addition, specific areas will be responsibility for supporting specific types of aims and objectives

Functional ethics refers to the ethics for functional areas of business like finance, human resource, marketing, etc. It focuses on specific ethical guidelines for various functions within a company. All functional areas within an organisation should establish ethical standards.

## 5.3 Types of Ethics According to Functions of Business/Functional Ethics

Most businesses consist of a number of different departments, each of which has a specific job or task to do - these are called 'functions'. Functional ethics covers the innumerable practical ethical problems and phenomena which arise out of specific functional areas of companies or in relation to recognised business professions.

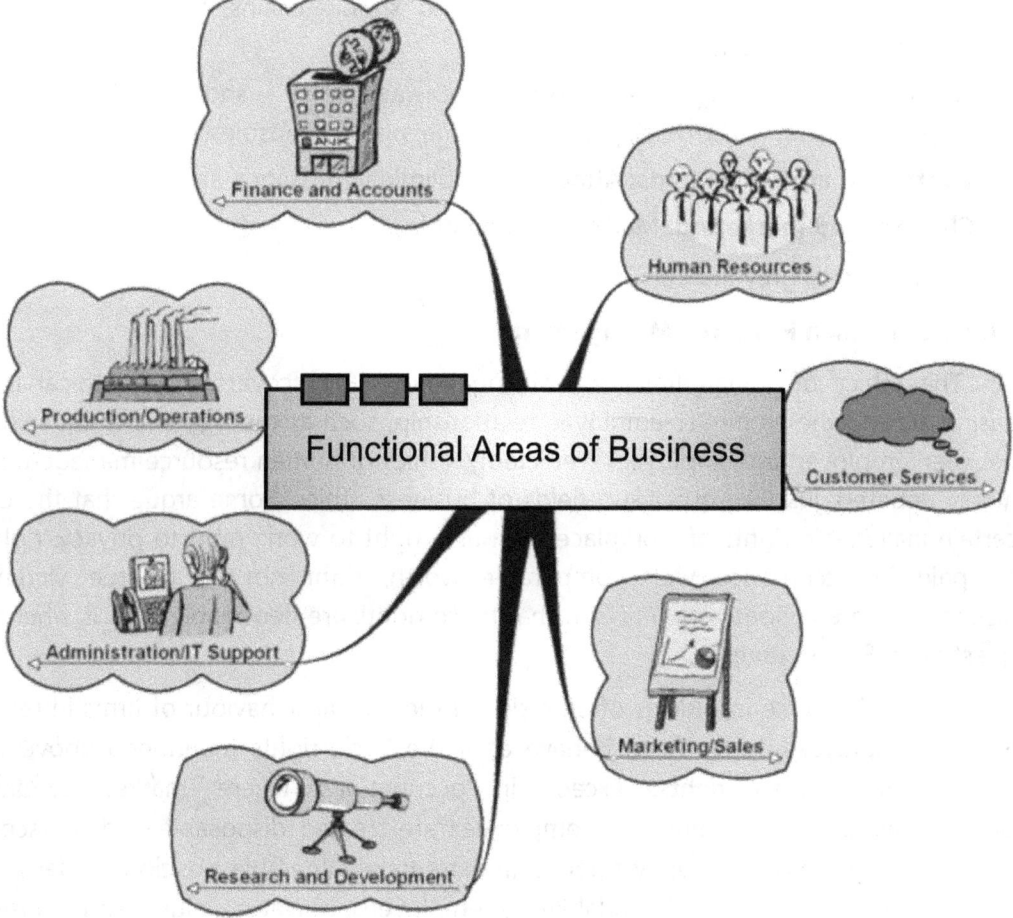

**Fig. 5.1: The Functional Areas of a business**

There are different types of ethics according to the various functions of a business. These are enumerated below:

1. **Ethics of Marketing**

    Ethics of marketing are the basic principles and values that govern the business practices of those engaged in promoting products or services to consumers. Sound marketing ethics are typically those that result in or at least do not negatively impact consumer satisfaction with the goods and services being promoted or with the company producing them.

    Marketing which goes beyond the mere provision of information about (and access to) a product may seek to manipulate our values and behaviour. To some extent society regards this as acceptable, but where is the ethical line to be drawn?

    - **Pricing:** price fixing, price discrimination, price skimming.
    - **Anti-competitive practices:** these include but go beyond pricing tactics to cover issues such as manipulation of loyalty and supply chains. See: anti-competitive practices, antitrust law.
    - **Specific marketing strategies:** Greenwash, bait and switch, shill, viral marketing, spam (electronic), pyramid scheme, planned obsolescence.
    - **Content of advertisements:** Attack ads, subliminal messages, sex in advertising.
    - **Children and marketing:** Marketing in schools.
    - Black markets, grey markets.

2. **Ethics of Human Resource Management**

    The ethics of Human Resource Management (HRM) covers those ethical issues arising around the employer-employee relationship, such as the rights and duties owed between employer and employee. Predictably, ethics of human resource management is highly debated, just like other sub-fields of business ethics. Some argue that there are certain inalienable rights of workplace such as a right to work, right to privacy, right to be paid in accordance with comparable worth, right not to be the victim of discrimination etc. Some others claim that these rights are negotiable. This is where the question of Ethics comes in.

    Ethical discourse in HRM is often reduced the ethical behaviour of firms in relation to their employees. Many firms behave as if the basic rights mentioned above were charity rather than rights. Except in occupations where market conditions overwhelmingly favour employees, employees are treated disposable and replaceable and thus they are defenselessly trapped in extremely vulnerable positions as far as job security is considered. This expendability of employees, however, is justified in 'business morality' texts on the grounds that the employee too has the free will to leave a company midway in case another opportunity arises.

It is believed that since 'both employees and employers do in fact possess economic power' in the free market, it would be unethical if governments or labour unions 'impose employment terms on the labour relationship'.

Discussions of ethics in employment management practices include issues like policies and practices of Human Resource management, the roles of the Human Resource (HR) practitioners, the decline of trade unionism, issues of globalising the labour etc.

- Discrimination issues include discrimination on the bases of age (ageism), gender, race, religion, disabilities, weight and attractiveness, affirmative action, sexual harassment and so on.
- Issues surrounding the representation of employees and the democratisation of the workplace: union busting, strike breaking.
- Issues affecting the privacy of the employee: workplace surveillance, drug testing, privacy and so on.
- Issues affecting the privacy of the employer: whistle-blowing.
- Issues relating to the fairness of the employment contract and the balance of power between employer and employee: slavery, indentured servitude, employment law.
- Occupational safety and health.

## 3. Ethics of Purchase, Selling and Distribution:

Every day the media has reports of cases of bribery and unethical business practices that involves the purchasing of materials or services in almost every country in the world. Although we like to think that the people who determine contracts and purchasing agreements are fair and ethical, there are some that will accept coercion that may affect the award of contracts that are worth thousands of dollars to those that are worth millions of dollars.

a) **Purchasing Standards:** Every company will hold their employees to a purchasing standard that is put in place with processes, methods and rules to ensure that the procurement process is as fair as possible. However, the purchasing of materials and services is a process that involves the interaction of purchasing staff and potential vendors, which leads to personal relationships and contacts. A purchasing professional will naturally call a vendor they have personal knowledge of before they cold call other potential suppliers. The relationship between a company and their suppliers is one that is developed over a period of time and based on personal relationships.

However, the purchasing professional is duty bound to their employer to ascertain the best product or service at the best cost, in the timeliest fashion. Purchasing standards are in place to ensure that the needs of the company are foremost in any negotiations with potential suppliers. The first ethical standards for purchasing professionals were published by the Association of Purchasing Management in 1929.

b) **Actions of Suppliers:** Although we expect purchasing professionals to be as ethical as humanly possible, most companies have a sales department whose job is sell your product and that can means having contact with employees of potential clients, which could be purchasing or non-purchasing staff. These sales teams will have budgets to promote products with advertising souvenirs, such as pens, calendars, diaries, etc., or more tangible gifts such as lunches. In a number of studies on purchasing it has been found that almost all purchasing professionals accepts something from vendors, even if it as small as an item of stationary.

Although the majority of companies will require purchasing and non-purchasing employees to sign and abide by an ethics policy, smaller companies are less likely to either have or indeed abide by a code of ethics. Small business failure is high and it is vital for companies to win business, and that can come at the expense of ethics.

c) **Non-Purchasing Employees:** Although large companies insist on purchasing professionals strictly adhering to ethics codes, the same is not necessarily true for non-purchasing staff. In many companies purchasing is allowed by department heads or even line staff which by-passes the purchasing department all together. This means suppliers sales departments can target non-purchasing staff to gain sales where perhaps they have been rejected by the purchasing department. Much of this rogue procurement is never seen by the purchasing department as it either is paid for a department's cost centre or checks cut by the accounting department.

Rogue purchasing has two major drawbacks for a company. Firstly the spending is never funneled through the purchasing department so there is no way to know if the purchaser obtained the best price for the item. Secondly, the purchaser may have been unduly influenced to make the purchase; perhaps by gifts, personal relationship or even a conflict of interest. Rogue purchases can make up as much fifty percent of a company's overall spending for a year. If non-purchasing employees are restricted to minor or even zero purchasing, the company would be confident that the purchases were made in an ethical manner and the best product was selected based on price, quality and delivery time.

4. **Ethics of Finance and Accounting:** Finance is fundamentally a social science discipline. The discipline shares its border with economics, accounting and management. Finance is concerned with technical issues such as the optimal mix of debt and equity financing, dividend policy, and the evaluation of alternative investment projects, and more recently the valuation of options, futures, swaps, and other derivative securities, portfolio

diversification etc. Finance is often mistaken to be a discipline free from ethical burdens. However frequent economic meltdowns that could not be explained by theories of business cycles alone have brought ethics of finance to the forefront.

Ethics of finance is narrowly reduced to the mathematical function of shareholder wealth maximisation. In the sections devoted to 'Financial Ethics' in 'Business Ethics' books, ethics of financial markets, financial services and financial management are discussed. Fairness in trading practices, trading conditions, financial contracting, sales practices, consultancy services, tax payments, internal audit, external audit are also discussed in them.

Below are some areas of financial ethics:

- Creative accounting, earnings management, misleading financial analysis
- Insider trading, securities fraud, bucket shop, Forex scams: concerns (criminal) manipulation of the financial markets.
- Executive compensation: concerns excessive payments made to corporate CEO's.
- Bribery, kickbacks and facilitation payments: while these may be in the (short-term) interests of the company and its shareholders, these practices may be anti-competitive or offend against the values of society.

5. **Ethics of Production:** This area of business ethics deals with the duties of a company to ensure that products and production processes do not cause harm. Some of the more acute dilemmas in this area arise out of the fact that there is usually a degree of danger in any product or production process and it is difficult to define a degree of permissibility, or the degree of permissibility may depend on the changing state of preventative technologies or changing social perceptions of acceptable risk.

    - Defective, addictive and inherently dangerous products and services.
    - Ethical relations between the company and the environment: pollution, environmental ethics, carbon emissions trading
    - Ethical problems arising out of new technologies: genetically modified food, mobile phone radiation and health.
    - Product testing ethics: animal rights and animal testing, use of economically disadvantaged groups (such as students) as test objects.

6. **Ethics of Intellectual Property, Knowledge and Skills:** Knowledge and skills are valuable but not easily "ownable" objects. Nor is it obvious who has the greater rights to an idea: the company who trained the employee or the employee themselves? The country in which the plant grew, or the company which discovered and developed the plant's medicinal potential? As a result, attempts to assert ownership and ethical disputes over ownership arise.

- Patent infringement, copyright infringement, trademark infringement.
- Misuse of the intellectual property systems to stifle competition: patent misuse, copyright misuse, patent troll, submarine patent.
- Even the notion of intellectual property itself has been criticised on ethical grounds: see intellectual property.
- Employee raiding : the practice of attracting key employees away from a competitor to take unfair advantage of the knowledge or skills they may possess.
- The practice of employing all the most talented people in a specific field, regardless of need, in order to prevent any competitors employing them.
- Bioprospecting (ethical) and biopiracy (unethical).
- Business intelligence and industrial espionage.

7. **International Business Ethics:** The issues here are grouped together because they involve a much wider, global view on business ethical matters. While business ethics emerged as a field in the 1970's, international business ethics did not emerge until the late 1990's, reflecting the international developments of that decade. Many new practical issues arose out of the international context of business. Theoretical issues such as cultural relativity of ethical values receive more emphasis in this field. Other, older issues can be grouped here as well. Issues and subfields include:

- The search for universal values as a basis for international commercial behaviour.
- Comparison of business ethical traditions in different countries.
- Comparison of business ethical traditions from various religious perspectives.
- Ethical issues arising out of international business transactions; e.g. bioprospecting and biopiracy in the pharmaceutical industry; the fair trade movement; transfer pricing.
- Issues such as globalisation and cultural imperialism.
- Varying global standards - e.g. the use of child labour.
- The way in which multinationals take advantage of international differences, such as outsourcing production (e.g. clothes) and services (e.g. call centres) to low-wage countries.
- The permissibility of international commerce with pariah states.

## 5.4 Patents, Copyrights, IPR, Trademarks and Business Ethics

**Intellectual Property** is defined as property that is the result of creativity and does not exist in tangible form such as patents, copyright, trademarks, etc. Intellectual property rights are like any other property right. They allow creators, or owners, of patents, trademarks or copyrighted works to benefit from their own work or investment in a creation.

**World Intellectual Property Organisation (WIPO)** is an organisation established in 1967, and an agency of the United Nations from 1974, for co-operation between governments in the matters concerning patents, trademarks, copyright, etc. and the transfer of technology between countries. Its headquarters are in Geneva.

## Copyright

It is a branch of intellectual property law - because it protects the products of people's skill, labour or time. Generally, it protects only literary, dramatic, artistic or musical work, sound recording, film, broadcast, or typographical arrangement. The main test is to confirm that some work or effort must have gone into it. A clear cut distinction is made here as while there is **no** copyright in facts, news, ideas, or information, copyright **does** exist in the **form** in which information is expressed and the **selection** and **arrangement** of the material because all these involve skill and labour. Interestingly, brief slogans and catchphrases have been ruled to be too trivial to be protected by copyright.

Copyright may be defined as the exclusive legal right, given to the originator or his or her assignee for a fixed number of years, to print, publish, perform, film or record literary, artistic, or musical material and to authorise others to do the same. It is also used to refer to the material protected by copyright.

Literary work is protected by copyright as soon as it is recorded in writing or otherwise. It includes newspapers and the writing that goes into them. When outside contributors supply material for publication to newspapers, whether paid or not, copyright will be owned by the contributor. Even reader's letters, sent to the newspaper, have by implication licensed it to use their copyright work on one occasion, and therefore, still retain their copyright.

Copyright, patents, intellectual property rights, trademarks are areas of unsettled legal and moral conflicts, and in the coming years, will surely absorb the mental energies, persuasive talents and intellectual acumen of future generations.

**Copyright in Speeches:** Copyright is given to spoken words (even when they are not delivered from a script) as soon as they are recorded, with or without the speaker's permission. The speaker, as the author of a literary work, will own the copyright on his words, unless he is speaking in the course of his employment. Reporting current events may involve the use of the record of the words spoken; but there will be no infringement if the record is a direct record and not taken from a previous record or broadcast; if the authority of the person lawfully in possession of it has been obtained for its use; if the speaker did not prohibit the making of the record; if it did not infringe any existing copyright; the use of the record was not of the kind prohibited by the speaker or copyright owner.

A speaker cannot prohibit the reporting of his words on second thoughts. He must prohibit the note or tape being taken before the speech itself, or clearly indicate how he does not want them to be used in a certain way, for example, in a newspaper.

Courts have laid down that reproducing substantial part of the speech infringes the act. Substantial part, however, does not refer to the length, but refers to the quality or importance of the material reproduced as well as the quantity or length.

In reporting parliamentary or judicial proceedings no copyright is infringed.

**Owner of the Copyright:** The first owner is the author. But in the case of work done in the course of employment, the employer is the owner, subject to any agreement to the contrary. The copyright of works submitted for publication by a freelance is always owned by the freelance contributor. Even if the work is ordered from a non-member of the staff, no automatic right accrues to the newspaper or magazine or periodical, to the copyright of the work.

**Copyright of Photographs:** When commissioned from a freelance or commercial photographer, copyright is owned by the photographer or his employer, unless there is an agreement to the contrary. The person who commissions a photograph for private or domestic purposes has the right **not** to have copies of the photographs issued to the public even if he does not own the copyright.

**Ethical Rights:** The Berne Convention gave moral rights to authors of Copyright work. These rights are as follows:

(1) The right to be identified as the author,

(2) The right not to have his work subject to derogatory treatment, and

(3) The right not to have a work falsely attributed to him.

The first two rights come under a restriction. They do not apply to any copyright work created for publication in a newspaper, magazine, or periodical, or to any work made available for such publication with the **consent** of the author. Nor do they apply to any other work done in the course of employment.

**Fair Dealing:** If a copyright work (apart from a photograph) is used for the purpose of reporting current events and is accompanied by sufficient acknowledgement of the work and its author, it is considered as "Fair dealing" and does not constitute infringement. "Fair dealing" is also attributed to the use of a copyright work (including a photograph) for the purposes of criticism or review of that work or of another, provided sufficient acknowledgement is made. However for broadcasting, the necessity for acknowledgement is dispersed with.

This is permitted as this allows for reporting which quotes from books, plays, films, other publications, or when writing a criticism, story or feature.

Copying which prevented the copyright owner from gaining financial benefit would also be ruled out. If more of the work is quoted than is necessary in reporting current events or in criticism or review, this may not be fair dealing. The photographing of the whole or a substantial part of a television image is restricted. The whole gamut of cyber crimes dealing with pirated productions is mind-boggling in its impact on the future of civilisation.

**Advantages of Copyright**

1. **Right to Produce/Reproduce:** Copyright gives the creator of a piece of intellectual property (This includes Literary, Musical, Dramatic, or Artistic work; not ideas) the sole right to produce and reproduce their work.

2. **Right to Authorise:** These rights include the right to authorise others to produce or reproduce your work as well as the right broadcast your work.

3. **Protection:** Copyright prevents your work from being stolen or misused by others.

4. **Moral Rights:** Copyright allows the holder of the copyright to object to uses of their work that they find morally objectionable.

**Disadvantages of Copyright**

1. **Inability to Share Work:** Copyrights key advantage is also its primary disadvantage. Copyright does not allow you to openly permit others to use your work or to distribute it, even if they are not doing it for profit. This can mean that your work is disseminated slowly or not at all.

2. **Authorship is not Ownership:** You must own the copyright to be able to exercise the rights that it grants, and just being the creator of the work does not always guarantee ownership. In some cases the owner is actually the person who commissioned the work, or the company for whom the work was produced.

3. **No Provision for Parody:** Copyright law does not allow for parodying of work without permission. Copyright law does not make a distinction between using a work for commercial or non-commercial purposes.

**Trademark**

It is a device, word, or combination of words secured by legal registration or established by use as representing a company, etc. It represents a distinctive characteristic identifying it as unique, or as the only sole thing of its land.

Trademark protection ensures that the owners of marks have the exclusive right to use them to identify goods or services, or to authorise others to use them in return for payment. The period of protection varies, but a trademark can be renewed indefinitely upon payment of the corresponding fees. Trademark protection is legally enforced by courts that, in most systems, have the authority to stop trademark infringement.

In a larger sense, trademarks promote initiative and enterprise worldwide by rewarding their owners with recognition and financial profit. Trademark protection also hinders the efforts of unfair competitors, such as counterfeiters, to use similar distinctive signs to market inferior or different products or services. The system enables people with skill and enterprise to produce and market goods and services in the fairest possible conditions, thereby facilitating international trade.

### Advantages of Trademarks

1. **Securing Exclusivity:**

   Registering your trademark is the quickest and most cost-effective way to ensure legal exclusivity for the use of your name or logo etc. Registering a trademark for your business or product name is similar to obtaining a certificate of title in relation to land.

   Registering your trademark significantly reduces the risk of being prevented from using your name or logo by other traders. One of the most emotionally draining and expensive things that can happen to anyone who owns a brand is receiving a "cease and desist" letter from a lawyer which requires you to stop using the name which you thought you owned.

2. **Geographical Coverage:**

   Registering your trademark usually gives you nation-wide protection instead of rights that are restricted to the specific areas or regions in which you trade.

   Further, if you want to expand overseas, this gives you a good platform to obtain rights in other countries – even before you commence trading in those countries.

3. **Deterring and Preventing Others:**

   Trademark registration deters other traders from using trademarks that are similar or identical to yours in relation to goods and services like yours (referred to here as "conflicting trademarks"). This benefit manifests itself in a number of ways:

   (a) **Before other traders choose their brand names:** Being able to use the ® symbol puts others on notice of your rights, and being registered means that others can find your trademark when searching the official register before choosing to commence using a particular name. This makes it much less likely that they'll choose to use a conflicting mark in the first place.

   (b) **When other traders seek to register their brand names as trademarks:** Having your trademark on the register makes it likely that trademark examiners will refuse to register conflicting marks. If (despite this) another trader is able to convince a trademark examiner to accept the mark for registration, having a prior registered mark gives you a strong right to oppose the registration before it's officially entered on the register.

(c) **When you discover another trader using a conflicting mark in the market place:** Having a registered trademark makes it much easier, quicker and cheaper for you to prevent other traders from using conflicting trademarks. Often one or two "cease and desist" letters from your lawyer will be sufficient, but if it is not, the process of taking someone to court under the Trade Marks Act 1995 is much less expensive than the options for owners of unregistered trademarks.

4. **Protecting yourself from Infringement Claims:**

   If Atul is using his registered trademark, the Trade Marks Act 1995 gives him complete defence should a second person sue him for infringing registered trademark. In other words, as long as he is using his registered trade mark, he knows that he is not infringing the rights of any other traders.

5. **Controlling the Use of your Brand by Others:**

   Registering your trademark makes it a lot safer and easier to licence the use of your trademark to others (e.g. manufacturers, distributors, franchisees etc).

6. **Capturing the Value of what you Create:**

   Holding a registered trademark significantly increases the value of your brand to potential purchasers, and hence any purchaser of your business is likely to pay much more for the goodwill that you build up.

7. **Securing the Co-operation of Third Parties:**

   Registered trademark owners are much more likely to secure the co-operation of third parties in the protection of their rights. For example, Google will act to prevent traders from bidding on "key words" that contain your registered trademark. Facebook may remove or reclaim user names that infringe your registered trademark.

**Patents**

A patent is deemed to be a government authority to an individual or organisation conferring a right or title, especially the sole right to make or use or sell some invention.

Patents provide incentives to individuals by recognising their creativity and offering the possibility of material reward for their marketable inventions. These incentives encourage innovation, which in turn enhances the quality of human life.

A patent owner has the right to decide who may – or may not – use the patented invention for the period during which it is protected. Patent owners may give permission to, or license, other parties to use their inventions on mutually agreed terms. Owners may also sell their invention rights to someone else, who then becomes the new owner of the patent. Once a patent expires, protection ends and the invention enter the public domain. This is also known as becoming off patent, meaning the owner no longer holds exclusive rights to the invention, and it becomes available for commercial exploitation by others.

**Advantages of Patents**

1. A patent gives the inventor the right to stop others from manufacturing, copying, selling or importing the patented goods without permission of the patent holder.
2. The patent holder has exclusive commercial rights to use the invention.

3. The patent holder can utilise the invention for his/her own purpose.
4. The patent holder can license the patent to others for use. Licensing provides revenue to business by collecting royalties from the users.
5. The patent holder can sell the patent at any price they believe to be suitable.
6. The patent provides protection for a predetermined period (20 years) which keeps your competitors at bay.
7. Patents are partially responsible for advancements in medical science, biotechnology, drug chemistry, computers etc.
8. Patents reward inventors with the aforementioned advantages and hence, create bigger and better discoveries.
9. With these benefits come certain drawbacks. Patents provide plenty of merit but are provided alongside certain conditions. These conditions can sometimes prove to be disadvantages.

**Disadvantages of Patents**
1. A patent is an exclusive right provided to a patent holder in exchange for the public disclosure of their invention. A full description with claims is published and can generally be viewed by anyone with the internet including your competitors.
2. After the exclusive patent period (20 years) has passed, other individuals or companies can freely use the invention without any permission from, or paying royalties to the inventor.
3. Applying for patent can be a very lengthy, time consuming process.
4. Cost of patent filing may be surpassing the actual financial gains. If a patent is to be filed further in different countries, then again the cost increases. After the patent grant, annual fees should be paid to the respective patent offices; otherwise the patent period may lapse.
5. You must be prepared to defend your patent if need be. Taking action against infringement is costly.

## 5.5 Ethical Challenges for Managers in the 21st Century

Managers in organisations face ethical issues every day of their working lives. There is seldom a decision they face that does not have an ethical dimension or facet to it. In addition to facing ethical aspects in their decision making, they confront ethical issues as they carry out their leadership responsibilities. Whether they be engaged in planning, organising, motivating, communicating, or some other management role, they face the fact that matters of right and wrong, fairness and unfairness, and justice or lack of justice creep into their decisions, actions or behaviours. Furthermore, it does not matter what level of management is under consideration - top, middle, or lower; managers at all levels, and in all functions, face situations wherein ethical considerations play a major role. The topic of ethics in management is a crucial one with which managers today must be informed.

Even though managers are faced with ethical issues, the issues differ from business to business. These ethical issues are as follows:

1. **Social and Environmental Responsibility:** In the 21st century, social responsibility has gained manager's attention. Ethical managers daily go through confronting ethical issues and knowing their responsibility as a manager and being confident in making the proper decisions. Now, consumers are demanding corporations to take full responsibility for the company's impact on community and the surrounding environment, more than ever. For ethical managers this presents confront on a daily basis. Ethical perspectives best suited to resolve such ethical issues is the common-Morality Theory because according to Beauchamp, Bowie, and Arnold, "there is a common morality that all people share by virtue of commercial life and this morality is ultimately the source of all theories of morality". The common morality is a set of norms shared by individuals who are committed to being free of any bias or prejudice based on facts of morality.

2. **Fraud:** Another ethical issue that managers face and can be very severe ethical violation within the company is Fraud. Ethical managers aware of dishonest activities within the workplace are required to report this to the appropriate authorities. This process is known as whistle-blowing. Most managers do not want to be a whistleblower, but reporting this to the appropriate authorities will maintain and promote an honest and fair workplace. The best ethical perspectives suited to resolve such ethical issues are the ethics of virtues. This approach according to Beauchamp, Bowie, and Arnold, "relies even more than does Kent's theory on the importance of having a correct motivational structure". Moreover, because this would be acting fairly and morally appropriate in acting justly.

3. **Diversity:** Organisations in the 21st century are like a society composed of many different cultures than it ever has been in the past. Diversity is another complex ethical issue managers confront because individuals from different cultures, and beliefs working together could cause many issues including discrimination, which could end up causing trouble for the business. Even though diversity can create possible ethical issues, it has many advantages to businesses, such as individuals from diverse culture could bring different sets of skills and strengths to the organisation that will allow the business to prosper. According to Sims, "As the twenty-first century approaches, companies face a variety of changes and challenges that will have a profound impact on organisational dynamics and performance". Ethical perspectives best suited to resolve such ethical issues are for ethical managers to ensure there are codes of professional practices, and society's moral standards and values are adhere.

4. **Discrimination:** Discrimination is another complex ethical issue that managers face at the workplace now more than ever before, due to the diversity in the work force and the chronological discrimination based on gender, race, ethnic origin, or sexual orientation lawsuits are serious. Charges could be filed against not just the company but possibly to the managers themselves. Ethical viewpoints best suited to resolve such ethical issues would be for the managers to ensure employees education about discrimination and avoid discriminating when hiring, promoting employees by basing on gender, race, or ethnic origin.

5. **Harassment:** The final complex ethical issue managers confront at the workplace is harassment. Harassment is morally and ethically wrong, but happens to many employees, from sexual comments to sexual advancements of the opposite gender. Best suited ethical perspectives for resolving such ethical issues would be for the managers themselves by addressing these issues in performance evaluations, and have a work out plan for a long-term solution.

6. **Health and Safety:** One area of ethical consideration for employers is how to balance expense control with the health and safety interests of employees. Manufacturing plants and other workplaces where employees use dangerous equipment or engage in physically demanding work should have strong safety standards that not only meet federal requirements, but that also makes eliminating accidents a priority. Even standard office workplaces pose health risks to employees who are asked to sit or stand all day. Unfortunately, certain organisations opt to cut corners on safety controls, equipment and training to save money. This is both unethical and potentially damaging in the long run if major accidents occur.

7. **Technology:** Advancements in technology and the growth of the Internet in the early 21st century have produced a slew of ethical dilemmas for companies. Company leaders have to balance the privacy and freedom of workers while also maintaining standards that require that company technology use is for legitimate business purposes. Certain companies go so far as to monitor all online use and email communication from employee computers and work accounts. A company may have this right, but its leaders need to understand the potential concern about privacy and autonomy among employees.

8. **Transparency:** Prominent business and accounting scandals have made it imperative that companies operate with openness and transparency. For public corporations, this includes honest, accurate and complete reporting on mandated financial accounting reports. For large and small businesses, transparency includes communicating messages, including marketing messages, that aren't open to misinterpretation and that clearly represent the intentions of the company and its messages. Being caught in a lie or avoiding full disclosure may cause irreparable harm to small businesses.

9. **Fair Working Conditions:** Companies are generally expected to provide fair working conditions for their employees in the business environment, but being responsible with employee treatment typically means higher labour costs and resource utilisation. Fair pay and benefits for work are more obvious elements of a fair workplace. Another important element is provision of a nondiscriminatory work environment, which again may have costs involved for diversity management and training.

Ethical managers face many challenge of ethical behaviour that they must confront if they are truthfully apprehensive about the survival and competitiveness of the business. In today's complex times businesses must step up, function with positive ethical cultures, and know how to deal with and resolve any ethical issues that come around. In order for ethical managers to stick to a high degree of ethical accountability and standards, they must be aware of their own individual ethical perspective and have an understanding of all ethical perspectives.

## Points to Remember

1. **Types of ethics according to functions of business are:**
   - Ethics of Finance and Accounting
   - Ethics of Human Resource Management
   - Ethics of Sales and Marketing
   - Ethics of Production
   - Ethics of Intellectual Property, Knowledge and Skills
   - International Business Ethics
2. **Intellectual Property** is defined as property that is the result of creativity and does not exist in tangible form such as patents, copyright, trademarks, etc.
3. **Copyright** may be defined as the exclusive legal right, given to the originator or his or her assignee for a fixed number of years, to print, publish, perform, film or record literary, artistic, or musical material and to authorise others to do the same.
4. **Trademark** is a device, word, or combination of words secured by legal registration or established by use as representing a company, etc. It represents a distinctive characteristic identifying it as unique, or as the only sole thing of its land.
5. A **patent** is deemed to be a government authority to an individual or organisation conferring a right or title, especially the sole right to make or use or sell some invention.
6. **Ethical challenges for managers in the 21st century:**
   - Social and Environmental Responsibility
   - Fraud
   - Diversity
   - Discrimination
   - Harassment

## Questions for Discussion

1. Explain the term "functional areas of a business". What are functional ethics?
2. What are the types of ethics according to the functions of business?
3. What is a copyright, patent and trademark?
4. What is meant by intellectual property rights?
5. Who owns the copyright in the following cases?
   - A newspaper reporter covering a function and producing a report on the same.
   - A freelance writer sending in his copy:
     (i) When solicited by the newspaper; (ii) unsolicited.
   - A photograph commissioned by an individual.
6. Discuss the ethical challenges faced by managers in the 21$^{st}$ century.

❑❑❑

# Case Studies

## 1. Integrity and Professional Behaviour

A junior member of staff has just returned to work after taking special leave to care for her elderly mother. For financial reasons she needs to work full-time. She has been having difficulties with her mother's home care arrangements, causing her to miss a number of team meetings (which usually take place at the beginning of each day) and to leave work early. She is very competent in her work but her absences are putting pressure on her and her overworked colleagues. You are her manager, and you are aware that the flow of work through the practice is coming under pressure. One of her male colleagues is beginning to make comments such as "a woman's place is in the home", and is undermining her at every opportunity, putting her under even greater stress.

**Question :**

1. How should you proceed so as not to discredit yourself, your profession or the practice for which you work and at the same time maintaining integrity and **confidentiality** in your actions?

## 2. Honesty and Integrity

Jayanth is a son-in-law of a local MLA and is now posted as block development officer in his father-in-law's constituency. He comes to know that MLA's followers, who are mainly small contractors and many elected members of Gram Panchayat, are hand in glove with local Panchayat officials in misusing MGNREGA funds. He finds that each Panchayat secretary along with elected members have used machines to complete many works under the scheme and siphoned off funds using fake job cards. He also finds out that all this was done at the behest of his father-in-law, the local MLA. Now, the state government has taken cognizance of the issue after a media report and has ordered inquiry into the scam.

Jayanth has to probe the matter and file a report to higher authorities. His father-in-law is pressurising him to file a false report as he himself is under pressure from his followers, who if found guilty will be slapped with a criminal case. Some contractors have contacted and requested him to not to mention their names in the report in return for a hefty bribe.

Some Panchayat secretaries have requested him to spare them as according to them Panchayat members had coerced them into becoming partners in crime. Jayanth is recently married and it is his first government job.

**Question :**

1. What should be his course of action?

## 3. Ethics in Public and Personal Relationship

Keshav recently got a job of First Division Assistant in Tehsil (Taluk) office. He is smart and hardworking. Because of which Tehsildar has become fond of him and though he is Keshav's superior, he has made Keshav his good friend.

Keshav is married to Ramya who is educated and recently got posted as Panchayat Secretary, incidentally to the Panchayat office located in Keshav's village itself. Ramya's mother-in-law is not supportive of her and her job. She frequently taunts Ramya and demands all of Ramya's salary to be given to her. Though Keshav supports Ramya, he seldom objects to her mother's remarks to his wife.

A young, male Panchayat member of same Panchayat where Ramya works, and who wields considerable clout in the village and Tehsil, comes to know that she had 'illegally' signed a property assessment certificate and claims that he has documents to prove his claim. The certificate was obtained by a relative of this Panchayat member who was not in good terms with him. In the past serious fights were taken place between them over this property.

Ramya insists that she signed it only after Panchayat's bill collector surveyed the property and gave his verbal assurance about the legality of the property in question. As he was born and brought up in the village and knew matters of the village very well, Ramya had trusted him. Now the Panchayat member is threatening her to take the matter to District Panchayat and get her suspended.

Ramya seeks her husband's help who is close to tehsildar and who in turn is a close friend of Block Development Officer. Ramya's mother-in-law is forcing her to quit the job and stay at home, but Ramya wants to be financially independent and pleads her innocence. Keshav is in moral dilemma over the entire episode.

**Question :**

1. What should be Keshav's course of action so that he doesn't compromise his ethics in personal and professional relationships?

## 1. Case Study 4

Rajendra is a reputed structural engineer and is working for a major metro rail project. He is in charge of design, construction and positioning of pillars of metro flyover.

A junior engineer in his team tells him that there is a major flaw in two erected pillars supporting a section of the flyover and they should be replaced/readjusted at any cost. These two pillars supported a flyover curve and if collapsed, it would cause a major accident and put many lives into danger. Moreover, in few days it is to be inaugurated for trial runs.

Rajendra brushes aside the apprehension and warning by his junior. But later in the evening, on second thought, he once again scrutinizes his plans and drawings, and finds that his junior was indeed right.

Accepting his mistake would tarnish his reputation for Rajendra. If any accident happens, which is certain to happen at certain point of time in future, it would affect the reputation of the company that constructed it. It will embarrass the government too.

Also, replacing the pillars would inflate the cost for the company and would further delay the project.

**Questions :**

In this situation:

1. What should Rajendra ideally do?
2. What would be the legal and ethical consequences of Rajendra's continued silence?
3. What are the qualities that are tested in this case study? Examine.

## 5. Case Study

Shalini has been recently hired full time at a major tech company where she interned for two summers during her college career. Shalini loves her job and has established many strong relationships with her co-workers over the time she has worked there. The company encourages the interns and new hires to interact with VPs and upper management in order to create an open and friendly atmosphere.

During her time as an intern, Shalini began to notice that one of the VPs paid her extra attention. When he was around he would always make an extra effort to stop by Shalinis cubicle and chat: something he did not do with any of the other interns. He reached out to her over social networking sites and even invited her to a gathering at his house. Some of her co-workers began to make offhand comments to Shalini about the extra attention.

Now that she was in a full time position, Shalini began to dread that she would soon have to work with this VP directly. While he has not done or said anything explicitly inappropriate, the extra attention - and the fact that her co-workers noticed it - made her very uncomfortable and undermined her concentration on work. When she was hired, she was told that she should always speak to her manager if she was uncomfortable or had issues with the work environment. While at the same time, she is afraid to come across like a tattletale since the VP hasn't explicitly done anything wrong.

**Question :**

1. What course of action should Shalini take?

www.ingramcontent.com/pod-product-compliance
Lightning Source LLC
Chambersburg PA
CBHW080351170426
43194CB00014B/2756